HEIDELBERG

Of the Norfolk 17

Robert D. Gaines
Andrew Heidelberg

Hidden Shelf Publishing House
P.O. Box 4168, McCall, ID 83638
www.hiddenshelfpublishinghouse.com

Heidelberg

Artist: Megan Whitfield

Graphic design: Ali Kaukola

Interior layout: Kerstin Stokes

Publisher's Cataloging-in-Publication data

Names: Gaines, Robert D., author. | Heidelberg, Andrew I., author.
Title: Heidelberg of The Norfolk 17 / Robert D. Gaines and Andrew
Heidelberg.
Description: McCall, ID: Hidden Shelf Publishing House, 2023.
Identifiers: ISBN: 978-1-955893-18-3 (paperback) | 978-1-955893-19-0
(Kindle) | 978-1-955893-20-6 (ebook)
Subjects: LCSH Heidelberg, Andrew I. | School integration--Virginia--
Norfolk--History--20th century. | African Americans--Education--Virginia--
Norfolk. | BISAC BIOGRAPHY & AUTOBIOGRAPHY / Personal
Memoirs | BIOGRAPHY & AUTOBIOGRAPHY / Cultural, Ethnic
& Regional / African American & Black | BIOGRAPHY
& AUTOBIOGRAPHY / Social Activists | BIOGRAPHY &
AUTOBIOGRAPHY / Sports | HISTORY / United States / 20th Century
HISTORY / United States / State & Local / South (AL, AR, FL, GA, KY,
LA, MS, NC, SC, TN, VA, WV)
Classification: LCC LC214.23.N75 G35 2023 | DDC 379.2/6309755521--dc23

Table of Contents

Introduction

I was a bit nervous when I first knocked on Andrew Heidelberg's door.

"I don't remember you in high school," he snarled, quickly followed by a grin. "That's probably a good thing."

He slapped my shoulder and warmly welcomed me into his home. I was there to write a book about my famous classmate at Virginia's Norview High School ... he wanted a movie. We would spend four years with interviews, writing, editing, a few misunderstandings ... and good times. Be warned, collaborating with Andrew Heidelberg was always riveting, never easy.

For starters, there was Andrew. Ever the gigantic personality, he was quick-witted, fun, interesting ... still running six miles every day at dawn into his seventies. That said, he was also hard-headed and occasionally mistrusting ... commendable considering the scars forever lodged in his heart and mind. Thankfully, Andrew's wife, Luressa, could act as referee when needed.

Andrew wanted to call the book *The Andrew Heidelberg Story* by Andrew Heidelberg as told to Bob Gaines. Maybe my name would be on the front cover, maybe not.

We both loved *The Colored Halfback* ... what the newspapers had first called him. It would be our working title. The problem was we didn't want readers to think the book was only about football. It's much deeper ...

We began writing around 2008, nearly fifty years after the Norfolk 17 accomplished what many, at the time, had thought near impossible ... busting segregation at six public schools. If getting there had been a war, being there was horrendous.

Frightening? In classrooms, white bullies pelted the Black kids with spit wads and slurs. Teachers looked the other way, either bigoted or simply afraid to take a stand. The hallways were worse, the bathrooms near deadly.

The Norfolk 17 may have courageously busted down the door, but opportunity remained locked and guarded.

It was not hard getting Andrew to talk openly about himself. He thrived in the spotlight, often using humor to disguise bitterness.

"I was called *nigger* a thousand times a day," he laughed.

Whoa, stop right there. Keeping in step with modern political correctness, what do we do about the *N-word*?

"We stay true to 1962," he demanded. "People, dialect, facts, culture. No way we gonna soften the shit."

Andrew seemed most concerned about reaction from the living members of the Norfolk 17. After all, he had managed a "football hero's pass" others were never afforded. That is partly why we wrote the story in the third person, to give the story a width beyond what was going through his mind at the time.

It was important—for historical accuracy—that names remain the same. Andrew definitely wanted to print the real names of those who had tried to humiliate him.

"Revenge," he quipped.

Eventually, we decided to adjust the names of several of the worst offenders at Norview. We didn't need to mention names of the racists he faced on the football field.

"I couldn't tell one of them from another," he joked. "I just focused on the game. Besides, I'd already heard all the words in the hallway. Those white punks just enhanced their vocabularies with shoves and fists and kicks. Hell, I might have even been tickled a few times. It was dangerous under that pile ... or anywhere on that field."

Mostly, they had a hard time catching him.

"A few of those guys looked me up over the years and apologized. I accepted ... glad they finally found their manners."

There was also the matter of the many white kids back then—including myself—who watched and did nothing.

"Bobby Gaines, I know you were hiding somewhere behind that swarm of bigoted assholes giving me shit all day." He playfully poked me in the chest with his finger. "You were young, stupid, and probably too damn scared to offer an opinion." He stopped poking me. "Anyway, I saw what happened when a white kid was branded a 'nigger lover.' If God, in all His glory, had accidentally made me white, I'd have probably kept my mouth shut too."

By the way, Andrew never had a problem with a white man being the writer.

"It's important that you were there," he assured me. "You know the feel, the time, the basics of what happened. And you're good with words."

Of course, he followed with a warning.

"Never forget it's my story, my life ... I own it."

Fasten your seatbelt ...

– Robert D. Gaines

Chapter 1

September 22, 1961

*A*ndrew Heidelberg stood alone ... anxious, defiant.

Once again, he had drifted into the center of the universe, the suspect of 11.000 white stares. Some were curious, others prayed for his very destruction.

Andrew smiled.

For a moment, he heard the Norview band, already lost in its music, but his mind was racing too fast to process sound.

And all was silent, the sun now swallowed by darkness, the tidewater air with its soothing muggy warmth just beginning to feel the invasion of fall.

Andrew pulled back, glancing quickly at the entirety of the packed stadium, white against the night. His gaze stopped at the newly established colored section at the far end of the visitor's side. Outside the fences, young black children excitedly weaved reckless paths through the old folks, locked in a moment they never believed possible.

On the home side of Chittum Field, white kids and adults, most decked in blue and white, all stared in the same direction, watching intently that one movement as number 33 prepared for battle, seemingly unconcerned that his life might end within the hour. They were the curious.

Hatred came from the other direction, the visitor's side of the stadium splotched with the threatening jeers and racist jokes of modern-day Virginia.

"Fuckin' nigger shouldn't be out there," blurted an angry man in his fifties, certain that more would agree. They did.

"Hey coon, we gonna eat you alive," yelled a student, his friends laughing and making jungle noises in unison.

"So, which one of dem Norview players is da nigger?" another kid bellowed, the visiting crowd now roaring in delight.

Of course, not everyone was loud. Some were just stunned—too much, too fast, too weird.

In the press box, Bill Piersall, long-time sportscaster for WNOR radio, cleared his voice as he checked out the Norview cheerleaders, twelve beautiful girls shaking blue pom-poms to the beat of the big band. Piersall noted the enormity of the crowd as he fiddled with his microphone, glanced at the roped sections of Black people, and scanned some of the large banners stretched across the stadium, each proclaiming victory and allegiance to the almighty god of Norview Pilots football.

On the field, the Pilots, wearing their all-white uniforms with the cool, blue-striped bars across the shoulders, surrounded Coach Charles McClurg for last-minute instruction. McClurg, a tall and stoic man in his early forties, seemed much older to his players, particularly with his classically unstylish suit and fedora hat.

"You focus, you work," said McClurg with unquestionable command. "You never tire, you never doubt your confidence. If you play team football, you win."

The Pilots roared in agreement.

Across the field, the Princess Anne coach gathered his players.

"Okay, there's been a lot of crap about this game," yelled the coach over the noise of the crowd and two large bands, "but I only want you to pay attention to our team. I want hard-nosed, take-no-prisoners football. I want you to knock these guys off their throne. I want you to leave them in mud and blood. Men, are you right for the fight tonight?"

The team responded, shoving their hands into a circle while jumping and shouting, their fans erupting with approval.

The broadcaster tapped his mike and turned the switch.

"Welcome to the WNOR game of the week. This is Bill Piersall, and we've got a dandy tonight, the 1961 season opener between the defending State and Eastern District football champion' Norview Pilots and the visiting Princess Anne Cavaliers. We're at Chittum Field, home of the Powerful Pilots, where the focus is not only on Norview's 36-game winning streak but mainly on one player, Norview's 150-pound colored halfback, number 33, Andy Heidelberg. Tonight, before a standing-room-only crowd of more than 11,000 fans, Heidelberg will become the first Negro to play football at a previously all-white high school in the state of Virginia and, I've been told, possibly the entire South. This historical moment has been both applauded by some and, quite frankly, angrily questioned by many. How will these two teams respond to this monumental challenge to Virginia and Southern tradition? We'll see because the Pilots are sending Heidelberg deep to receive the opening kickoff."

Piersall paused, immediately breaking back with a heightened tempo.

"And, folks, you certainly won't have any problem finding number 33 on the field. Andy Heidelberg looks, as the saying goes, like a fly in buttermilk."

Piersall chuckled over the air, impressed with his clever quip. But he was quite right. Andrew Heidelberg, his black skin shining from within the pure white uniform, was helmet-to-helmet with a teammate.

"I want you to run your ass off tonight," shouted senior running back Calvin Zongolowicz as he grabbed Andrew's arm. "Remember, we're behind you."

Heidelberg nodded his head up and down, giving Zongo a brief smile as Piersall continued his commentary from the booth.

"And we would be remiss," he said, "if we didn't mention what some folks have been wondering. Will the Norview players even care to block for Andy Heidelberg?"

As the Pilots took the field, the noise of the crowd hit full throttle, cheers finally managing to cloak the taunts. Andrew moved to the mouth of the goal line as the Princess Anne players huddled over the ball, the captain moving his head to the center of the group with the last word before kickoff.

"Let's break every bone in that skinny nigger's body," he barked.

The Cavaliers reacted with passion and excitement as they spread across the 40-yard line for the opening kick.

Standing alone at the end zone with two Norview players about 10 yards in front of him, Andrew glanced into the sea of white. Once again, sound was blurred by focus.

"Gimme the ball," Andrew said to himself.

It was always that way.

Chapter 2
Chesapeake Manor (1957)

By the shape of the dirt and grass, this just might have been the one hundredth game of the summer on the neighborhood football field, otherwise known as Oakwood Elementary School's front lawn.

Andrew grabbed the high kickoff, looking quickly at the herd of 13-year-olds bearing down for the hit. He immediately gauged the possible blocking from his own teammates, as if that really mattered. He cut right, juked the closest potential tackler, and broke clear, sprinting through the blur of laughter and screams on his way to another score, talking loudly as he crossed the makeshift goal line.

"And number 33, Ollie Matson, scores again," bellowed the skinny kid with the lightning moves. "Da Chicago Cardinals keel the Washington Redskins, hah."

The jabbering and arguing heightened as Andrew placed the ball on the ground and turned around to give an instantaneous impression of Chuck Berry.

"Just let me hear some of dat Rock and Roll Music," warbled Andrew, known in these parts as Bird. "Any old way you choose it. Got a back beat you can't lose it, any old time you use it."

Knuck, known by older folks as Bobby Wilson, was the first to congratulate Andrew in the end zone.

"Bird, when you gon learn you caint sing," said Knuck, breathing hard and strong after the long run. "You can thank me for my block gettin you tada end zone. I was right behind ya."

"You was way outta bounds, Bird," yelled one of the sore losers from the other team. "Ain't no football field dat wide. And Knuck was holding me."

Bobby looked puzzled, dramatically gesturing with his arms.

"I was what?" he blurted. "I wont holdin you, sucker. And I knocked yo butt outta bounds. Is yo chest still hurtin?"

Ignoring the cries for a penalty, Bobby announced the score.

"Dat makes it 60 to 36. We kickin yo butt, suckas."

"Ya'll ain't got no 60 points, nigga," yelled an opponent. "You caint count dat last one."

"I can and I did," yelled Bobby as he and Andrew headed back for the next kickoff.

Bobby turned to his best friend.

"Wit my blockin, Bird, you might make it to the pros."

"Well, you better get mo speed, Knuck," answered Andrew with a big grin, "cause I caint be waitin on ya."

It was on ...

"Listen, Bird," snapped Bobby. "You better learn how ta wait for your blockin or somebody gon break yo neck. I can see yo butt flyin in da stands when Sam Huff hit ya."

As Andrew knelt to hold the ball for Bobby's boot, Knuck cupped his hand to his mouth as if he was a sportscaster.

"And there he goes, sports fans, number ..."

Bobby held the last syllable.

"Bird," he said, "what number you gon be wearin when you git knocked out?"

"Number 33, man, Ollie Matson," Andrew bellowed as if Knuck

should not even need to ask. "Cept it gonna be Heidelberg number 33, da Baltimore Colts' scoe-in machine."

"Oh, now we're playing wit da Colts," said Bobby. "Don matter to the Redskins cause dey got nothin but white boys, and they gon be tryin to kill yo butt. But I caint help yo no moe, Bird, cause I'm gon be playin baseball with da Dodgers."

From 20 yards downfield, the opposing players were becoming irritated by the delay.

"Kick da ball, man," yelled Johnny. "It's gettin late."

Andrew, a look of sudden shock, stood straight up, leaving the ball unattended.

"Oh no," he gasped. "Hey Knuck, what time is it?"

"It's gotta be almost six o'clock," said Bobby, knowing his friend was late again. "You better git a move on it, man, and get home fo da colonel kick yo butt."

Without hesitation, Andrew took flight.

"Gotta go, man," he yelled as he darted toward home. "See you guys later."

****

Andrew ran from the field to his home. He didn't want to upset anyone, so he moved at full speed. Briefly, the thought of his 15-year-old brother, Melvin, struck with a devastating ache. Andrew pushed his pace, his heart pounding hard. It had only been a month since Melvin had drowned, each of the Heidelbergs still deeply hurting, relying on faith and the strength of their family bond. Andrew ran harder, slowing down just enough to not burst through the front door. As he turned the doorknob and took a last-second breath, he was both surprised and relieved to see his mother and father in the living room with three visitors, two women and a man. The conversation stopped as everyone turned their eyes toward Andrew.

"Here's my son," said a beaming Mrs. Heidelberg. "Andrew, these people are here from the NAACP, and they have some questions they want to ask you."

Andrew took a few more deep breaths to recover from the dash home.

"Good evening," he said with a polite smile to acknowledge the guests.

Not only was Andrew breathing hard, but he was sweating profusely from both the summer heat and being inside the house.

"Hi, Andrew," said one of the ladies, smiling and taking a few deep breaths as if she were helping him recuperate. The stranger was quite attractive for a woman who was probably in her forties, tall and thin with uncommonly long fingers.

"As your mother said, we're from the NAACP," she said, her voice strong and words distinct. "I don't know if you've been keeping up with the news on the radio and TV about the integration of Negro children into the white schools in Little Rock, Arkansas. Or, if you heard about the Supreme Court ruling that segregation in the public schools is unconstitutional."

She paused to stare at Andrew, who was nodding his head to show understanding.

"So," she continued, "you have heard about the Negro children integrating schools in Little Rock?"

"Yes ma'am," said Andrew, wiping the sweat from his face, glancing at his parents, and then focusing on the lady from the NAACP. She returned his smile, then looked toward the second NAACP lady, a younger and smaller woman who had seemed very anxious to join the conversation.

"Well, Andrew," said the second lady with a slightly higher ring and quick delivery that immediately made Andrew's head pull back. "While the Supreme Court has ordered desegregation in all the public schools in the South, whites round here have been working overtime to defy the law of the land. The white people have been hollering about states' rights and that Southern Manifesto. And yapping about their massive resistance to keep their schools lily-white. We're gonna keep fighting them with lawsuits. We're gonna stop Mayor Duckworth, that rebel Senator Harry Byrd, and all of them segregationists in Norfolk and Virginia. They ain't gonna stop our children from getting a good education, we guarantee you that."

"We don't know how long it'll take," the first lady added calmly, "but we know we won't give up, and we will eventually triumph. Right now, we're signing up Negro children to go to Norfolk's public schools. So far, we've registered quite a few who are brave, intelligent, and willing to help fight to integrate the white schools."

The man, the oldest of the three, clasped his hands together and leaned forward.

"And, young man," he said, "we're here today to ask if you might be interested in signing up to take part in all of this?"

Andrew did not even pause before giving his answer.

"Sure, I'll go to da white schools," he said. "I'll be glad to go."

All the adults seemed quite pleased as they looked and smiled at each other. The NAACP man took out some papers from a briefcase and began to give them to Andrew's father.

"That's wonderful, Andrew," said the NAACP lady with long fingers. "You'll be a real pioneer for civil rights. We'll give your parents more details, get you signed up, and we look forward to talking with you again."

"Yes ma'am, thanks," Andrew courteously replied while nodding his head and taking a few steps toward his room. "Nice to meet y'all."

As Andrew entered his bedroom, he heard the people from the NAACP praising his parents for raising such a fine and mature young man. It was obvious he had avoided the punishment for being late.

As he closed the door, Andrew spotted his favorite football card on top of his dresser. He picked up the Topps card of Chicago Cardinals' running back Ollie Matson, number 33.

"And dey fake da handoff to Matson," said Andrew as if he were a play-by-play radio announcer, "and give it to Heidelberg. Matson makes a block and Heidelberg breaks through da line. He's in da clear, dey'll never catch him now, he's gone. Another touchdown for da greatest player in the pro football history, Andrew 'da Birdman' Heidelberg."

Placing the Matson card back on the dresser, Andrew turned on his radio and carefully adjusted the dial to find the right reception. Perfect. As the sound of Fats Domino floated across the airwaves, Andrew instinctively moved his fingers with the piano, and his body followed. Blissfully harmonizing to *Ain't That A Shame*, he immediately stopped when his mother knocked on the door and entered the room.

"Son, I am so proud of you," she said, reaching for the radio to turn down the volume. "Like the lady said, you are going to be a pioneer."

"Yes ma'am," answered Andrew, pleased by his mother's excitement.

"Well, I gotta finish dinner," she said. "Gonna be a little late tonight, but that's okay, we got something to celebrate. Yes indeed, my son's gonna be a pioneer."

"Even if he's a dead pioneer," Andrew whispered to himself as he shut the door behind her and turned up the volume for Fats Domino.

****

Early the next morning, Bobby stood outside the Heidelberg's front door popping a baseball into his glove.

"Morning, Miss Lena," he said as Mrs. Heidelberg opened the door. "Is Andrew home?"

"Good morning, Bobby," she answered politely, then paused to put emphasis on her next two words. "I'm fine. And, yes, Andrew is home. Come on in."

"Andrew," she called loudly toward her son's bedroom, "Bobby's here."

Mrs. Heidelberg listened for a response, but could only hear the noise from Andrew's radio, Frankie Lymon and The Teenagers singing *Why Do Fools Fall in Love*.

As she picked up her purse from the kitchen table, she yelled again, this time much louder.

"Andrew, turn down that radio, Bobby is here."

The sound of the music diminished.

"Ma'am?"

"Get out here right now. You got company."

As Mrs. Heidelberg opened the front door to head for work, she turned to Bobby.

"I thought y'all were playing football," she said. "Have you switched to baseball now? I can't keep up with y'all."

"Yes ma'am," answered Bobby as Andrew entered from his bedroom, the music having been settled to a moderate blare.

"Hey, Knuck, what's up?"

Bobby had no time to answer since Mrs. Heidelberg was already talking.

"Andrew, you better make sure this house is straightened up before you leave. And turn that radio off before you go."

Shaking her head and smiling, she turned her attention to Bobby.

"Boy listens to that music all day long," she grumbled before turning one more time to Andrew.

"And make sure you lock my doors, you hear me?"

"Yes ma'am."

She opened the door, then stopped again.

"Bobby, make sure that boy locks my door."

"Yes ma'am, Miss Lena," answered Bobby as she closed the door.

"What's up with da baseball stuff?" said Andrew. "I thought we was playin football?"

"After you went runnin off last night, we all decided we'd play a real sport."

Bobby tossed the ball to Andrew, who caught it with one hand and flipped it back before hurrying to his room to get his glove and click off the radio.

"Let's go," said Andrew as he locked the front door. "Hey, throw da ball."

Tossing the baseball high in the air toward his friend, Bobby doubled back to see if the door really was locked.

"C'mon man," said Andrew as he threw back the ball.

The boys hardly noticed the late summer heat and humidity of morning as they played catch while walking up Denison Avenue, finally approaching Sewells Point Road.

"Hey Bird," said Bobby, "did da colonel kick yo butt when you got home last night?"

"Naw, man," answered Andrew. "Dem NCAAP people was here last night."

"NAACP people? What dey want?"

"I'on know," said Andrew, "sumpin bout signin up people to go to da white schools."

"Da white schools," repeated Bobby, rather surprised. "Wit white kids?"

"Yep," said Andrew.

"Whatchu tell em?"

"I told em I'd go."

"You kiddin me?"

"Naw, I was just tryin ta keep my daddy mind off beatin my butt," said Andrew. "Den I said I'd go."

Bobby was still stunned.

"What about Booga T?"

"Man, you know I wanna go to Booga T," said Andrew, "but I guess dey want me ta go ta Norview."

Bobby started to chuckle.

"C'mon, Bird, you know dem white people ain't gon let no colored people walk in der white schools. Not Norview, not nowhere. Man, we caint even go to da Southern Shopping Center without havin to run like hell to get back home. Dem whiteys gonna kill you boy if you go ta Norview, specially da many times you throwed rocks at em."

Both boys let out haughty laughs as Andrew raised his open hand to make a point.

"Thank God we fast, huh Knuck?"

"Yep," agreed Bobby with a huge grin as he pretended to run in slow motion. "We way too fast for dem white boys."

Bobby stopped and looked seriously at Andrew.

"So, Bird, you really told em you would go?"

"I told em I'd go," said Andrew. "But I ain't even worried, cause dem NAACP people are crazy. Who dey think wanna go to dem white schools and git lynched anyway? Besides ..."

Andrew stopped to confirm his point, pronouncing each word slowly as if revealing an unbending law of life.

"Ain't no niggas goin to school wit white people in Norfolk,

Virginia. Ain't gon happen, cap'n."

The boys finally reached Sewells Point Road, looking to cross into Oakwood. They stopped as a souped-up 1949 Ford approached and slowed. Inside were four white teen-aged boys. Except for the driver, they began beating loudly with their hands on the side of the car, yelling at Bird and Knuck as they passed by.

"Hey niggers, get off the road," one of them laughed.

Instinctively, Andrew and Bobby both flipped the finger at the white boys.

"C'mon, crackers," yelled Bird, "get outta da car and see what happens."

The car screeched its brakes, stopped momentarily, then moved quickly in reverse. With his torso stretched out the car's back window, the nearest white boy had something in his hand.

"Take a shower, niggers," he yelled while hurling a balloon full of liquid that splashed just short of the boys' feet. Amidst laughter from within, the car took off, its tires squealing. Still flipping off the enemy, Andrew and Bobby quickly crossed the road into the safety of Oakwood.

"Did dey git cha, Knuck?" said Andrew, looking for any wetness. "Was dat water or piss?"

"Hell naw, Bird, dat's definitely piss," said Bobby. "And you wanna go to school with dem mothas?"

"No way, man," said Andrew. "I hate dem crackers. I hate em."

****

Andrew Irwin Heidelberg had lived his entire life in Norfolk. Born November 6, 1943, he was delivered in his parent's apartment at Oakleaf Park. With three boys, the Heidelbergs soon moved to Cumberland Street in the heart of downtown Norfolk's Black neighborhoods and businesses. In the late 1940s, they lived in a small house on Olney Road with two rooms and no indoor toilet.

In 1951, the Heidelbergs moved to the new rental housing development in Oakwood known as Chesapeake Manor, surrounded by the colored sections of Rosemont, Chesapeake Gardens, and Mamie Properties. Their beautiful single-story apartment at 900 Denison Avenue had a kitchen, living room, two bedrooms, and a bathroom. It was a wonderful home.

****

Andrew had never known any white people and his encounters, for good reason, were always distant.

His first vivid white memory was wedged in his mind as if it had been played to a national audience and forever noted within the unpublished book of Black history. Every movement of that memory was permanent, the haze of time blurring the background.

It was a Saturday morning, Mrs. Heidelberg taking the three boys downtown to the Norfolk Tabernacle. Andrew was almost 8, Melvin 9, and Kenny 11. Having recently moved to Chesapeake Manor, they had to take the yellow and red Virginia Transit Authority bus to Church Street. They would transfer at Tidewater and Lafayette to a VTA bus—crowded with white people—that traveled through upper middle-class white neighborhoods. On this Sabbath, Mrs. Heidelberg and her boys found a seat near the middle of the bus, their manners and eyes under quiet control. At the next stop, two young teen-age white girls boarded.

Andrew barely noticed as the girls stood at the front of the bus, looking for a seat. The driver, a grumpy middle-aged white man, stood and scanned the rows, a look of indignity as he spotted the four Heidelbergs.

"Get up," he ordered, no further explanation needed.

As Mrs. Heidelberg and her three boys vacated the seat to stand in the aisle, the two girls confidently claimed their prize.

Andrew was stunned, embarrassed, and angry, his young mind pushed to full speed. His mother, a grown woman, forced out of her seat for two arrogant white teenagers. What kind of world was this? They were on their way to church, for heaven's sake. Did not God see this absurd injustice? Was there nothing that could be done?

Whites? Andrew learned early that the races in Virginia did not mix, and never would.

Chapter 3
Summer of '58

Bobby and Andrew were walking along Sewells Point Road in the direction of Norview High School. To the east was the Oakwood section where Bobby lived, to the west was Andrew's home in Chesapeake Manor. Although both areas were entirely Black, there was a distinct difference.

Oakwood was a thickly wooded area that engulfed a scattering of small shanty houses. There were no paved roads, plenty of ditches, and still a few outhouses. Bobby's home resembled a small double-wide trailer but was quite comfortable and did have plumbing.

Chesapeake Manor was strikingly different. In 1950, most of the woods had been cleared for several hundred apartments and a few single homes. The project had paved roads and sidewalks with brick structures that were organized on many large, well-defined lots.

The Heidelbergs lived at the corner of Dennison Avenue and Gregory Drive, the two main streets of the neighborhood. Theirs was the end dwelling of four one-story structures that were linked together, the beginning of a U-shaped configuration that included eight double-story and four single-story apartments, all sharing a large, manicured grass field with concrete walkways. This was replicated on additional pieces of land that spanned to the edge of the elementary school.

Even though the cinder block apartments were somewhat spartan in appearance, they were modern and comfortable. To the kids who lived there, the family-oriented environment of Chesapeake Manor was a true paradise with plenty of room to play.

Although they attended the same school, the Chesapeake Manor and Oakwood boys were divided by a well-known animosity, a partition based on sidewalks and indoor toilets. It was perceived that the "urban" Chesapeake Manor boys looked down on the "rural" Oakwood boys. Of course, because of the perception, they did. And, occasionally, the subtle resentment erupted into accusations, taunts, scuffles, and fights.

Several years after the Heidelbergs had moved to Chesapeake Manor, Andrew tried out for a baseball team, not knowing, or caring, that most of the players were from Oakwood. He knew many of them from school but had never seen Bobby, who attended St. Joseph's Catholic in downtown Norfolk. After the first practice, a couple of the older kids, aimed at stirring trouble, secretly took Andrew's glove and tossed it into the woods. When Andrew questioned where his glove had gone, the boys told him that they had seen Bobby heave something into the woods. Although Andrew immediately realized that the older players were hoping to instigate a fight, he was agitated and stormed toward Bobby.

"Hey, did you throw my glove into da woods?"

Taken by surprise, Bobby looked hard at the new kid spitting anger.

"Man, I ain't throw no glove in no woods."

"Dey say you did," argued Andrew as he pointed to the group

of older boys, the villains trying not to laugh.

"I ain't throw yo glove nowhere," Bobby shot back. "An dat's dat."

Andrew stared into Bobby's eyes, his fists unclenching.

"Okay," he said.

"I help ya look for it," said Bobby.

The search was quick. The older boys, partially out of guilt and mostly because the intended fight was not going to happen, pointed to the location and Andrew retrieved his glove. That was the beginning of what would certainly be a lifelong friendship. Besides, Bobby and Andrew were the best players on the team. Bobby—who could hit, throw, and play any position better than anyone else on the team—was born to be a Major League star. Andrew—the fastest kid on the team—was a great hitter, strong infielder, and second pitcher behind Bobby, who often kidded Andrew about having a "weak arm."

In truth, Andrew could not match Bobby's incredible baseball talent. For the sake of argument, however, Andrew would forever claim he was, at the very least, just as good as his best friend. When Bobby disputed, as he always would, Andrew turned the argument up a notch.

"Knuck, you wanna race to decide who da best? I be touchin home an you be trippin on second."

Andrew, by his own words, was the "king of baseball."

Plus, without any doubt, he was better at football, no matter what Bobby might say.

****

Now, as the soft and muggy summer began to fade, the two continued their assault on playing sports, talking sports, harmonizing to hit songs, and trying to stay out of trouble.

"Hey, Knuck, did you hear Jimmy Best is startin a Junior League football team out here," Andrew blurted with excitement. "I caint wait. Um gon play quarterback, you know dat."

"I know you gon run da ball ery play," Bobby shot back. "Dat's cause you ain't gon pass it ta nobody, cause you ain't got no arm anyway."

"I can pass good enough," Andrew disputed, "but Jimmy Best say he need a smart quarterback, an somebody who can scoe at any time. Dat's me."

Andrew stopped, bent over an imaginary center and called the signals: "Ready. Set. Hup one, hup two, hup three."

He faded back as if looking to connect on the long pass to Bobby, who instinctively ran a pass pattern across Sewells Point Road. Andrew hurled the pretend pass—a perfect spiral—with Bobby making a spectacular catch.

"Hey, Bird, let's take Johnston Road," said Bobby as Andrew ran across the street well ahead of an approaching car, that was suddenly slowing down to a crawl, filled with white boys.

"Watch out, niggers," one of them yelled as he raised his arm out the window to flip the expletive, his hand stiffening for the exclamation of hate.

Andrew, his body language pronounced with indignity, returned the gesture as Bobby picked up a rock and swiftly fired it at the car, the baseball-sized rock bashing loudly into the rear fender.

"Whoa," yelled Andrew as both boys looked at each other in hearty surprise, then quickly made their escape down Johnston Road. The white teens did not follow. About 100 yards into the safety of the colored territory, Andrew and Bobby slowed down.

"I dare em to come in here," said Bobby, his breath reeling from the explosive run and laughter.

"Man, you can really throw," said Andrew. "I keep forgettin

26

baseball is yo thing."

"Um glad you know dat, Bird," said Bobby. "It's good you finely admit dat you ain't da only star on da planet."

"What you talkin bout," grumbled Andrew. "I said you was good at baseball, I ain't say you was good as me."

Once again, puzzled by Bird's outright stupidity, Bobby put both of his hands confidently on his chest.

"Dat ain't even no question, Bird."

Now Andrew played the victim.

"Dude, I'll bust yo ass in football and baseball," he said before pretending to dribble a basketball, stopping to swish a jump shot.

"And den I'll stop by da basketball court," bragged Andrew, "and hit nothin but net in yo eyes."

Andrew continued his imaginary dribble, jamming his butt into his friend's leg and spinning to shoot another fade-away jumper, Bobby now jumping high for the mythical block.

"Not today, nigga," jabbered Bobby. "Dat all you got?"

"I got more," growled Andrew.

"See bout dis," boasted Bobby, moving quickly into baseball by assuming the pitcher's stance with an arrogant glare for Andrew.

After shaking off the first sign, he nodded approval for the pitch.

"Hit dis heat, Bird," said Bobby as he began his wind-up and fired the make-believe fastball.

Andrew took a hearty swing, looking into the far sky as he watched the ball go deep.

"Dat ball is headin for da fence," said Andrew. "Whoa, its outta here. Heidelberg with da grand slam homerun ... game over."

"Ain't nothin but a foul ball, Bird. No balls, two strikes, and you bout to go down swingin."

"Naw, man, it was fair all da way," giggled Andrew as he knocked an imaginary football out of Bobby's hands, yelled fumble, and started to run. Except now Bobby yanked the ball out of Andrew's grasp.

"I got it now, man," proclaimed Bobby.

"Na way, Knuck. Dat was my shadow you was tryin ta tackle," taunted Bird as he headed for another touchdown.

****

Neither Andrew nor Bobby bit into the Oakwood versus Chespeake Manor rivalry. They were best friends and that was all that mattered. Always welcome, they spent many weekends and summer nights with sleepovers at one home or another, each an honored guest to caring families.

****

Almost late, Andrew opened the door to find his father reading the newspaper, mother cooking dinner, and older brother, Kenny, setting the table. It seemed just another dash into normalcy, except ...

"Andrew," his mother beamed as if the greatest kid in the world had just arrived home.

"Yeah, Momma?"

"Guess who stopped by today?"

"You dead now, turkey," chuckled his brother with the sly grin of impending disaster.

"Shut up, Kenny," Mrs. Heidelberg commanded to the bad son before returning her smile toward Andrew.

"You know Miss Evelyn Butts, the lady who lives in Oakwood and works with the NAACP?"

Mrs. Heidelberg waited for Andrew to reluctantly nod his head.

"Well, she came by and told me to get you ready to go to the white school."

Andrew looked stunned.

"Huh?"

"What you mean, 'huh?' A 'yes ma'am' or 'no ma'am' works fine."

"Yes ma'am."

Mrs. Heidelberg continued, her happiness ignoring Andrew's look of bewilderment.

"Anyway, Miss Butts said that the white folks are still trying tactics to keep us outta them schools with their massive resistance and all that other racist garbage, but the NAACP believes we're real close to you attending Norview."

"But, Momma, I was plannin on goin ta Booga T," said Andrew in obvious pursuit of sympathy.

Mrs. Heidelberg did not buy the drama, her voice rising an octave with every reason why she was totally right, and he was totally wrong.

"Why would you want to go eight miles over town on the bus to school when you can walk to school for nothing and save us $1.25 a week? Besides, Booker T been there since I was born, and it is fallin' apart. Now, you can walk right down the street to a new school that got everything?"

"Cause all my friends are goin ta Booga T," said Andrew as if she might buy a different argument.

She didn't.

"Well, not all of them," she countered. "The NAACP said they signed up 150 children, so you'll have plenty of company."

"I hope so," said Andrew, barking softly with indignity, saving his best reason for last. "Cause I sho don feel like gettin lynched by myself."

"Boy, ain't nobody gonna lynch you," said Mrs. Heidelberg.

"Oh yeah, I bet Emmett Till's momma said da same thing. Dey pulled him outta his house, dragged him down da steps ..."

Mrs. Heidelberg abruptly interrupted.

"Boy, shut up with that stupid talk. You got Emmitt Till on the brain and that ain't healthy. Believe me, I wouldn't send you up there if I thought somebody was gonna hurt my baby."

"I ain't no baby, Momma," said Andrew, his head slightly bowed in frustration as he tried to move past his mother, who extended her arms for a hug.

He was trapped.

"You're still my baby," she said softly with a smile as she squeezed the embrace and gently patted his back. "Now, wash your hands. Dinner's ready."

"Yes ma'am," said Andrew as he broke free.

"Told ya you was dead," his brother giggled.

"Kenny," snapped Mrs. Heidelberg, "I ain't telling you again.

Chapter 4
The Dead Life of Emmett Till

Andrew sat on the edge of his bed, his eyes burning with intensity and knowledge.

"Man, dem white men came and took Emmett Till outta his own house one night and dragged him in da car," he said in a heightened whisper. "Den dey took him in da woods and gouged out his eyes for just looking at a white woman. Den dey beat his head wit a hammer over and over til you couldn't even recognize him. Den dey shot him in da head and dumped him in da river with a fan wrapped around his neck. Dey don't be playin, man, when it come to talkin to a white woman."

Bobby was shocked.

"Man, I heard dey lynched him, but how'd you know all a dat?"

"Knuck, it's right dere in *Jet Magazine*," said Andrew as he reached under his bed to retrieve the evidence. "Let me show ya da picture."

Andrew pulled out the magazine, easily finding the page that told the story of Emmett Till.

"Man, dey got da picture right here," said Andrew. "Check dis out, Knuck."

"Damn," said Bobby, shaking his head in disbelief. "I betcha

31

won e'er see me talkin ta no white girl."

"Knuck, I'on even believe you know no white people, do ya? And I ain't countin dem white boys dat been throwin pee at cha."

"You right, Bird. I'on know none and I'on wanna know none, dat's fa sho."

Still philosophical, Andrew offered his friend some well-founded advice.

"I tell ya one thing, Knuck. When da white folks say hello, you better have dem rocks in yo pocket."

****

Andrew, his mind replaying a recent touchdown, was in the backyard taking clothes off the line. As he started to take an armful into the house, his mother rounded the corner while reading a letter.

"Andrew, this letter is from the Norfolk School Board. It says y'all have to be at John Marshall School next week to take a test."

"A test?"

"Then you get to meet with the School Board for an interview," she continued.

"A what?"

"An interview, Andrew."

"Why I gotta do all dat?"

"I don't know, Andrew. I'm not making the rules. If you don't take the test, you ain't going to Norview."

His arms still full of clothing, Andrew prepared himself for one more stand.

"Momma, I told you I changed my mind."

Of course, he knew she wouldn't budge. She put her hands to her side and looked straight into his eyes. As expected, her voice was uncompromising.

"I don't think I heard what you said, boy."

"Do I have to go?"

"You don't have to do anything, Andrew Irwin Heidelberg," she said in a voice already proclaiming victory, "but I wouldn't want to be in your shoes if you don't."

Mrs. Heidelberg walked back into the house, Andrew in pursuit, quickly dropping the clothes on the living room chair.

He was down to his last feeble plea.

"But why do I have ta take some dumb ol test?"

Mrs. Heidelberg stopped.

"I guess they wanna know if you're smart enough to go to school with their white children."

Andrew started walking toward the back door.

"I'm smart enough," he said with disgust. "Ain't no doubt about dat."

As he closed the screen, he could hear his mom's loud response from inside the house.

"And don't let nobody tell you nothin' different," she bellowed.

She came to the door as Andrew began taking some more clothes from the line.

"If you wanna play football this afternoon," she said, "I suggest you finish bringing in the clothes. And make sure you fold them ... neatly."

"Yes ma'am," said Andrew, his day totally ruined.

****

Andrew was bored, his mom stoic. The bench was hard, the hallway without character. A few other kids and their parents also sat and waited for the school board interview. Andrew squirmed, his mom giving him a stern look and restraining tap. This was his second venture into the white world in less than a month, the first being the test he had to take several weeks back with 151 kids all trying to act like sitting inside a white school was not totally creepy. But, as strange as that place had been, this was worse.

"How long we gotta sit here?" he whispered, the uncalculated minutes having numbed his mind and body. "That stupid test was easy, but I got a bad feelin bout dis."

"First, we will sit here until they call you in," said Mrs. Heidelberg. "Second, do you remember what I told you? Talk slowly and speak clearly. It's *this*, not *dis*. And you ain't got no bad *feelin* ... you got a bad *feeling*."

"Exactly," he said with perfect English. "An extremely bad *feeling* ..."

Andrew put his head into his hands and continued to squirm, despite the pokes from his mom. Time could not be more agonizingly slow.

The door to one of the rooms opened again, another kid and her parent exited. As the white man prepared to announce the next name, everyone in the hall prayed it might be their turn.

"Andrew Heidelberg," the white man called.

Finally.

Andrew and his mother got up from the hard bench and walked toward the man, who silently nodded his head without expression. Andrew was not sure whether he was nervous or had simply lost all feeling in his stomach. He tried to swallow.

The large room was about as dull as the hallway, except for the many pictures of old white men hanging on the walls.

Andrew and his mother were asked to sit at the large table across from three men, members of the Norfolk School Board. They each had a pile of folders and cleared their throats in a very official manner. A fourth white man sat at the head of the table, behind a plaque that read: Mr. E.L. Lamberth, Assistant

Superintendent of Schools, General Administration. Like the other three, Mr. Lamberth had no expression as he shuffled through his folder of papers. No one offered a greeting.

Suddenly, Mr. Lamberth looked up at Andrew.

"Well, Mr. Heidelberg," he said, "tell us why you want to go to Norview."

Andrew instinctively knew that when a white person called a colored person "mister," trouble usually followed. Still, he did not hesitate to answer.

"Because everything they got at Norview is ten times better than what they got at Booker T."

Mr. Lamberth appeared shocked at how quickly and precisely Andrew had responded. He looked back down at the papers in his folder, then stared at Andrew.

"Ten times better, Mr. Heidelberg? How do you know that?"

"Well, I know the school is new and I know the football team and the baseball team got real pretty equipment and their uniforms and stuff is new," he answered, feeling strangely confident. "Over at *Booker* T, the uniforms are old and the field don't look nothin ... excuse me, nothing like Norview."

"Well, you know, Mr. Heidelberg, you won't be playing any sports at Norview," said Mr. Lamberth.

Andrew was stunned, slightly sick. What kind of nonsense was this?

"No, sir, I didn't know," said Andrew, somehow hoping that Mr. Lamberth was mistaken. And, even if the superintendent was correct, an exception would certainly be made considering Andrew just might be the best football player on the planet.

Mr. Lamberth raised his thick eyebrows, which seemed to have more hair than his thinning buzz cut. Again, he looked at his paperwork before lowering his voice for the attack.

"Well, your fifth-grade teacher at Oakwood Elementary, a

Miss Brown, says here that you always want to be the leader or the big shot, that you want to be first in everything. And she adds that, at times, you are quite sassy."

"No sir, I'm not sassy," Andrew shot back in a tone that all four white men—by their callous expressions—undoubtedly considered sassy.

"That was not a question, Mr. Heidelberg," said Mr. Lamberth, his voice even more commanding and somewhat angry. "It was a statement. This Miss Brown does go on to say you were a very bright student and you had previously attended a private school?"

Andrew remained quiet.

"That was a question, Mr. Heidelberg. What private school would you go to?"

"Bank Street Baptist Church, sir, starting in the first grade," said Andrew, realizing what he should have known all along, that Mr. Lamberth was not his friend. "I went there for three years and Miss Williams said I should be skipped to da ... the fifth grade even though I was only eight, so I already knew most of the stuff dey ... they studied at Oakwood. Miss Brown got mad at me for talking in class, but it was the other kids asking me questions."

Mr. Lamberth put his hand up to silence Andrew and looked at Mrs. Heidelberg.

"A private school for Negroes. What would that cost?"

"It was $2 a week, sir," she said, trying to appear friendly, but burning inside at the inquisition.

Mr. Lamberth gave a distant and somewhat arrogant smile, portraying a deliberate look of superiority as to how good a $2 school could possibly be. He made a note on his paper and looked back at Andrew.

"Mr. Heidelberg, I will tell you I am somewhat concerned

about your behavior," he said.

Mrs. Heidelberg could not help but move to her son's defense.

"If I might say, sir," she said, "my son knows how to behave. He's a good boy."

"He had better be," said Mr. Lamberth, "because there will be no sassing at Norview."

He turned again to Andrew, his eyebrows still expanding.

"You will not be a leader," he said. "And if you do try to win at everything, you will only be making enemies. I'm telling you this, probably for your own safety, stay out of trouble. Let the white kids be the leaders and let them win. Do you understand, Mr. Heidelberg?"

"Yes sir," said Andrew, understanding precisely what Mr. Lamberth was ordering—be an obedient and easy-going nigger. Mr. Lamberth looked around the table at his colleagues and, for the first time, gave a courteous smile toward Andrew and his mother.

"Thank you, both," he said, not offering to shake hands.

****

As the Heidelbergs escaped the stodgy old building, Andrew was comforted by the hot air of Norfolk. What a relief, it was over. But after walking a few feet from the building, Mrs. Heidelberg grabbed his arm, pulling him toward her.

"Boy," she said strongly. "If you intentionally let anybody beat you doing anything at Norview, I'll beat your hind-parts myself. You hear me."

"Yes ma'am," said Andrew, smiling appreciatively.

Chapter 5

Doin' That Crazy Hand Jive

*I*t was late afternoon of another long and hot summer day. Returning from her job cleaning the home of a wealthy white family, Mrs. Heidelberg unlocked the front door while mentally logging the whereabouts of her men. Her husband was probably heading home from the Norfolk Naval Shipyard, her oldest son was likely out trying to get one of the neighbors to let him wash their car, and Andrew was undoubtedly playing football, baseball or basketball with his friends, most likely at the field beside Oakwood Elementary School.

Putting her purse on the table, she approached the kitchen cupboard to start preparing dinner, pausing to turn on the radio. It was obviously Andrew's station, WRAP, The Silhouettes singing *Get a Job*. She listened for a moment, wiggled her body ever so slightly, then adjusted the channel to find the six o'clock news.

Pulling out some potatoes, she vaguely heard the daily update on the crisis in Lebanon and a nuclear submarine returning home from its trip under the North Pole. She did pay close attention to the news out of Arkansas, where the Little Rock school board, the state legislature, and Governor Faubus were closing three schools for the entire year to avoid integration. Mrs. Heidelberg shook her head and started to peel a potato as the radio station turned to local news.

"Addressing a U.S. District Court ruling to integrate, the Norfolk School Board last week tested 151 Negro students to determine academic and psychological readiness," the newscaster stated. "The board announced today that none of the students were qualified."

Mrs. Heidelberg set down the knife, rolled her hand over a partially peeled potato, and stared out the kitchen window.

****

It had been several weeks since the Norfolk School Board had decided that none of 151 colored kids, including Andrew, had the character or intelligence to attend the white schools. The official reasoning was that each child was not prepared and that their presence in a white environment would subject them to harm. Therefore, for their own protection, they should continue to attend the colored schools.

Answering the front door, Andrew's mother was surprised to see Marge Turner.

"Hi Marge, c'mon in," said Mrs. Heidelberg.

"Lena, you should have been at the courthouse today," said Mrs. Turner, quite excited. "Sorry you had to work ... you missed it, girl!"

"What happened?"

"Girl, Judge Hoffman let those crackers have it today," said Mrs. Turner, so excited she could hardly speak fast enough. "He was mad at the white school board for not accepting even one of the 151 children. It was something to see."

Mrs. Heidelberg was quickly getting wound up, as well.

"Go on, Marge," she said, her hands anxiously expressing her anticipation.

"Judge Hoffman asked them, 'Are you saying that you found none of the children qualified?' And the school board man said, 'That is correct, your honor.' Judge said, 'Were these children not accepted because of color?' He said, 'No sir, your honor.' And then the judge said, 'What if these children were white? Would they have been accepted if they were white?' And the man said, 'Yes, if they were white, they would have been accepted.' Judge said he had heard enough. He told them to get their ugly white faces out of their sorry white asses ... well, he didn't exactly say it that way. He did say, 'You will review those applications again and you will come back with a list of students acceptable and you will open those schools.' Judge Hoffman was truly angry, Lena. He's one of the good ones."

"The Lord is on our side," said Mrs. Heidelberg in great relief.

"But, Lena, you know those white racists will be pulling something sneaky again. Governor said he ain't gonna integrate, and that he's *obligated* to close all the schools. Oh, he also said that we are all a bunch of communists."

Mrs. Turner raised one finger to make a point.

"I ain't no communist," she continued with forceful expression. "I'm an American."

"You got that right," agreed Mrs. Heidelberg.

"Well, we should celebrate this day right now and be ready to fight again tomorrow," said Mrs. Turner, still indignant that her patriotism could possibly be questioned. "I gotta go, but just thought I'd stop by and tell you the good news. I'll see you soon."

"Thank you, Marge," said Mrs. Heidelberg as she closed the door.

****

The four family members sat at the dinner table, holding hands as Mr. Heidelberg said the prayer.

"Saying Amen ... blessing, and glory, and wisdom, and thanksgiving, and honor, and power, and might be unto our God forever and ever. Amen."

"So be it," they all repeated.

"And bless the hands that prepared this food," added Mr. Heidelberg as both boys smiled at their mother.

"Andrew, I had a call from the NAACP today," said Mrs. Heidelberg.

Andrew was immediately apprehensive.

"Yes ma'am?"

"The school board gave Judge Hoffman the names of 17 children they are acceptin' to go to the white schools," she said with a voice suddenly proud and excited.

Andrew's eyes widened as he prepared for the words he didn't want to hear.

"Ma'am?"

"Yep, 17," she said. "And guess what?"

Andrew winced.

"Andrew, you're one of the 17 they've chosen. You're goin' to Norview High School."

Andrew pulled back in his chair, slowly shaking his head sideways, his face with the look of impending doom.

"When?"

"When schools open, boy," she said. "In two weeks."

Kenny Jr. interrupted with a look of foolish concern.

"You okay, Andrew?" he quizzed. "Dog, Momma, he looks like he turnin' white."

Mrs. Heidelberg tried not to laugh, then noticed the change in Andrew's countenance and brushed off Kenny's remark.

"I guess we're going to be going to quite a few meetings

to see how the NAACP will set things up," she said. "There's another meeting tomorrow night at Miss Mason's house, so I'll probably know more after that."

"We got another meetin, already?" moaned Andrew.

Mrs. Heidelberg repeated his words with mock emphasis.

"*We* don't have anything, boy. I am the one who has been going to all the meetings? All you need to do is get yourself ready to go to school."

"You gotta scuse him, Momma," said Kenny. "He never been no white boy before."

"Ain't you supposed ta be goin ta da Army?" Andrew snapped at his brother.

"That'll be soon enough, Andrew," said Mrs. Heidelberg. "You're gonna miss your brother when he's gone."

"Only thing he's gon miss," said Kenny, "is da football."

As Kenny laughed at yet another one of his cool jokes, Andrew grabbed the change of subject and excitedly turned to his father.

"Hey, Daddy, Jimmy Best wants me to play quarterback on da new junior league team. We gon be da Crusaders."

Andrew stood up and pretended he was throwing a pass.

"Bobby gon play end and, you know, ain't nobody gon stop us. Um gon scoe a hun-erd touchdowns."

"Boy, sit down and eat your food," Mrs. Heidelberg scolded. "You're not playing football now. And where did you learn to talk?"

Mrs. Heidelberg acted like she was throwing a pass while imitating her son's phrasing.

"Um gon scoe a hun-erd touchdowns," she muttered slowly, pointing her finger at Andrew.

"I sure wish y'all thought about school as much as that old football," she continued. "I'm telling you again, you better get your lessons first or ..." Mrs. Heidelberg stopped in mid-sentence, again mimicking her youngest son. "... you ain't gon be playin nothin."

"Lena, leave the boy alone," said Andrew's father, "and let him have a little glory. He can do both."

"That's right, Daddy," said Andrew. "I'll get A plusses on all my tests and still ..." Andrew paused, then spoke each word slowly, with perfect pronunciation. "Score one hundred touchdowns."

"Boy, you talk too much," said Mrs. Heidelberg. "First, you get the hundreds on your tests, and then you can get your touchdowns. You hear me? I don't care what your father says."

"Yes ma'am, I will," said Andrew. "Can I be excused?

"Boy, get your taut-eyed self outta here," she said. "Whose turn is it to do these dishes?

"Kenny's turn," said Andrew as he took his plate to the sink. Kenny was suddenly his brother's best friend.

"Andrew, do the dishes for me tonight and I'll do them tomorrow."

"No way, man," said Andrew as he headed to the bedroom.

His brother grumbling in the distance, Andrew closed the door to their room and pulled the old *Jet Magazine* from under his bed, easily leafing to a page he had looked at a hundred times before.

Chapter 6
The Basement School

*I*t was the opening game for the Norfolk Colored Recreation Bureau's 1958 junior league football season at Barraud Park, the Crusaders already crushing the opposition. Both teams wore old and shabby uniforms that were far less attractive than those worn by kids in the white recreation league. Although most of the uniforms were too loose or too tight, no one seemed to care ... this was big-time, organized football.

Andrew, wearing number 12 this week, had done just as Bobby had predicted, run rather than throw, already to the tune of four touchdowns. He had thrown Bobby one pass good for a first down, but number 5 was open more than not and his buddy was barely looking much beyond his own daylight.

Coaches' Jimmy Best and Frank Becoate stood on the sideline, shouting encouragement. Best had started the team for the young boys in the Oakwood area, but had turned over the head coaching duties to Becoate, a young Navy sailor from South Carolina who had recently moved to Virginia. Becoate, who had played football in high school and the Navy, had no problem with Andrew scoring most of the touchdowns. Still, he didn't want him running the ball every play.

"Bobby was wide open that last play," Coach Becoate told Andrew on the sideline. "You wanna first look for the pass and then run if everybody's covered. But, hey, great touchdown."

A bit later, with Andrew back in the game calling signals, the bureau's director—Columbus "Joe" Austin—was talking to Coach Becoate on the sideline.

"Who's your quarterback, Frank?"

"That's Andrew Heidelberg, Mr. Austin."

Austin knew Andrew from rec league basketball and baseball.

"How old is he?" Austin asked.

"Only 14," laughed Becoate. "He's probably the youngest kid on the field."

Austin shook his head.

"Man, he's some player. But I don't care how young he is, he's too good for these boys. He probably should be playing in the senior league."

The fans sprinkled on all sides of the field would no doubt agree with Austin's assessment. Many were parents or siblings, but there were plenty of people just looking for entertainment on a warm evening in early fall.

Sitting under a tree on one of the park benches, an old man watched the action while listening to a small transistor radio. A newscaster was giving an important update about the six public schools in Norfolk that remained closed four days after they were supposed to open.

"Governor Lindsay Almond today granted the Norfolk School Board two more weeks to reach a solution to keep its schools segregated. If not, he said that the schools will be permanently closed, and all state funding halted. Adding that the mixing of the races will absolutely destroy public education, Governor Almond said it was his duty to the people of Virginia to close the schools rather than have them integrate."

Heidelberg

As the crowd cheered yet another Crusaders touchdown, the old man turned up the volume, pressing it closer to his ear.

"The lockout affects nearly 10,000 white students, along with 17 Negro children hoping to break the color barrier by integrating the six padlocked Norfolk schools. Meanwhile, in high school football, the closings will not affect Friday's season-openers with Norview the preseason favorite to win the Eastern District title."

****

After the romp, the Crusaders celebrated in one of the park's two dimly lit locker rooms. Bobby led the team in a wild song that would have made the Coasters wince with pride.

"Take out the papers and the trash," Bobby thundered as players banged on their lockers and sang in a blissful scream. "Or you don't get no spendin' cash. If you don't scrub that kitchen floor, you ain't gonna rock and roll no more ... Yakety Yak, don't talk back ... Yakety Yak, Yakety Yak ..."

The song continued for all four verses before Bobby returned to the beginning, only to be loudly quieted by Joe Austin.

"C'mon, you Oakwood girls, let's get a move on it," boomed Austin. "We got another game, and we need these pants and jerseys now. And take you stinkin' feet outta my shoes. Get em off, turn em in, and get outta here. And may I suggest that every one of you takes a shower when you get home. Man, for being such a good football team, you guys sure do smell."

****

The evening was starting to dim as Bobby and Andrew walked north on Tidewater Drive toward their homes, sticking out their

46

thumbs to hitchhike whenever a car approached.

"You a lucky mamma jamma, Bird," said Bobby.

"Whatcha talkin bout now Knuck?"

"Err'e nigga I know gotta git up in da mornin an go ta school, cept you," said Bobby, giving a disgruntled laugh. "I'm surprised yo momma and daddy ain't lettin you go to Booga T."

"I cain't go to Booga T, Knuck," said Andrew. "My momma say if we go back to da colored schools, dat's it ... da white people just gon open up der schools and say 'too late, you had yo chance, now stay in yo Black school.' My daddy say da white cracker's massive resistance is a sin."

"You know what I say, Bird," Bobby said. "White man caint lose wit da shit he use and niggas caint win for the shape dey in."

As both boys laughed, Bobby jabbed Andrew, his voice turning serious.

"Man, my momma say she don't think da gov'nor gon ever open dem schools for da niggas."

"Well," said Andrew, "I'on know dat dem NAACP people talkin bout startin a tutorin school for us at some church downtown."

"A church?" said Bobby. "Damn, Bird, good luck on dat."

Andrew shook his head.

"Wit da way things movin, Knuck," Andrew said philosophically, "I'm gon need mo den luck."

****

In the basement at First Baptist Church, Bute Street, it was the first day of the NAACP tutoring school, and Andrew, who should have caught an earlier bus, was late. The faculty, looking formal and well-educated, stood behind Vivian Carter Mason at the front of the large room.

"Good morning students, my name is Mrs. Vivian Carter Mason," she said in a soothing, eloquent voice. "I'm a member of the NAACP and the superintendent of our fine tutoring school."

Mrs. Mason was also an immaculate dresser.

"This school was set-up to serve as an educational conduit for you until such time that the white public schools open their doors to admit you," she continued. "Until then, I want to commend you all for your strength of character and your resolve to make this a better world. It is my esteem pleasure to introduce our principal, Mrs. Gertrude Perry."

Although approaching 80 years, Mrs. Perry was extremely sharp. After all, she had graduated from Harvard. And to prove her lofty intellect, she slowly pronounced each word with a very distinct Massachusetts accent containing perfect articulation and enunciation.

"It is an honor to be here," said Mrs. Perry to the 16 students who were not late. "I have studied each of your transcripts, and they are quite impressive. We are going to have a most wonderful and productive academic experience, and I am certain that you will have no trouble continuing the good work when you reach your various schools."

Finally, Andrew arrived, approaching from behind the other seated students as not to be noticed.

"Hello, Mr. Heidelberg," interrupted Mrs. Mason with a broad smile that signaled all the students and faculty to laugh. "Late on the first day?"

Andrew lowered his head, quickly found an open seat, and looked around the room in search of familiar faces. He saw his neighbor, Freddy Gonsouland, plus Pat Turner and her younger brother. Why didn't he ride with Freddy?

Mrs. Perry again addressed the class.

"Being a graduate of Harr-varrd University, I take great pride in the scope of my duties and, I will say ..."

Andrew stopped in mid-glance, his mind no longer listening as he eyes fell upon a beautiful female student.

As Mrs. Perry babbled something about intellectual curiosity and hunger for knowledge, Andrew continued to helplessly watch the most beautiful girl he had ever seen.

"Study tenaciously and always enunciate and articulate when you speak to anyone," Mrs. Perry concluded. "Mrs. Mason will now introduce your exceptional teachers."

"With the assistance of the NAACP," Mrs. Mason said, "we have assembled a brilliant faculty to assist in your preparation."

She introduced each teacher—Mrs. Arvella Howard (English), Mrs. Pecolia Jones (Social Studies), Miss Elizabeth Jones (Science), Mrs. Eleanor Dawley (algebra and geometry).

Andrew gulped, giving a wondrous stare at the young, gorgeous, and sexy Mrs. Dawley. But his gaze was only momentary, instead, turning his focus back to the beautiful classmate, praying she would be joining him at Norview.

"Mrs. Jackson will maintain your physical education requirements," said Mrs. Mason. "Spanish will be taught by the illustrious Dr. Rodolpho Cejas and Mr. Charles Corprew. And Mrs. Darby will supervise our studies in French."

Mrs. Mason led the students in short applause.

"With students in the seventh through eleventh grades, we expect each of you will give your best at all times. As I name your school, please stand, introduce yourself and state your grade. Let's start with Northside Junior High."

Mrs. Mason introduced one student from Northside, two from Blair, and five from Norview Junior High.

"And now the high school students," said Mrs. Mason. "We have one student going to Granby."

The beautiful girl stood.

"Hi," she said. "My name is Betty Jean Reed and I'm a sophomore."

It was like a hammer had smashed all hope. Granby? A sophomore? An older woman would never stoop to fall in love with a freshman. It wasn't fair. Betty Jean Reed ... what a beautiful name.

After Mrs. Mason introduced one student who would be going to Maury, she asked the seven who were headed to Norview to stand, motioning first to Andrew.

"My name is Andrew Heidelberg. We've already met."

The students chuckled.

"Andrew," said Mrs. Mason, "what grade will you be in at Norview?"

"Ninth grade, ma'am," he mumbled, hoping Betty Jean Reed would not hear.

"What's that?" Mrs. Mason asked.

"Ninth grade, ma'am," a bit louder, but still hurried.

"Yes, a freshman," Mrs. Mason said in a voice that bellowed over half of Norfolk. "Thank you, Andrew."

After all the introductions, Mrs. Mason wished everyone luck and asked if there were any questions. Freddy Gonsuland raised his hand.

"Yes, Mr. Gonsuland."

"Ma'am, if the white schools are closed, how come they're still playing football games?"

Everyone in the room, including Mrs. Mason, laughed.

"Because, Mr. Gonsuland, football rules the world."

****

In the basement at Bute Street, Superintendent Mason was addressing the 17 students, yet another motivational speech filled with non-violent suggestions should they ever be taunted

50

by whites.

"I expect each of you might be both excited and uncertain about the days ahead," she said. "This is a daunting task and some in the white community will be angry, but the entire nation will be watching, and you will be a shining example for the whole Negro race."

Andrew looked around the room at the other kids, his eyes once again finding Betty Jean Reed.

"As an opportunity to really get to know one another," Mrs. Mason continued, "the NAACP is treating us to a special weekend adventure. First, because we are at the forefront of desegregation, the Benevolent Protective Order of Elks would like to feature us in their 60th annual grand parade in Newark, New Jersey."

Andrew gave a contorted look to Freddy, who returned the wince. What could be so great about going to Newark?

"And then," continued Mrs. Mason, "we will head to Atlantic City for an evening of dinner and fun."

Okay, Atlantic City. Andrew and Freddy both smiled at each other. Now, this would be a trip.

"By the way," said Mrs. Mason, "people are already calling you the 'Norfolk 17.' Wear that title proudly."

****

The 60th annual Elks Parade—right through the heart of downtown Newark—turned out to be quite the event. Just ahead of a huge marching band, the Norfolk 17 float led the parade as thousands of spectators, nearly all Black, applauded and cheered wildly. As Andrew and the others, sitting in desks on top of the float, waved to the crowd, each realized, perhaps for the first time, that their efforts to integrate the schools of

Norfolk were making an impact far beyond their neighborhood. The pride Mrs. Mason had so often mentioned quickly took hold.

Andrew would wave, then glimpse at Betty Jean, radiant as always.

During the bus ride to Atlantic City, Andrew continued to watch Betty Jean, who was sitting near the front with her girlfriends, Johnnie Rouse and Carol Wellington. Andrew and Freddy had seats near the back of the bus with several of the guys. Andrew had long admired Freddy—he was athletic, handsome, smart, and a year older. While Andrew was the star of the junior football league, Freddy was tearing up the seniors. Had he gone to Booker T. Washington, he would probably already be a star halfback on the varsity.

"Hey Freddy," said Andrew, "you ever wonder why in the world the white school board picked us?"

"Nah man," said Freddy. "I don't think about it and I don't care. I'm just here, unfortunately."

"Well, I been thinkin bout it," said Andrew. "All dem 151 kids and dey only came up with 17 names. Um thinkin they picked out all da kids wit da craziest and funniest names you ever heard of so it wouldn't at least sound like we was niggas, huh? Look at me, Andrew Irwin Heidelberg."

Freddy looked away from the window and smiled.

"Yeah, you don't look like no damn German to me," he said, studying the lines of Andrew's face. "And you don't look like no Jew either."

"What's a Jew sposed ta look like?" said Andrew.

"I don't know," said Freddy, "but you don't look like one."

Now they were both laughing.

"And you don't look like no Frederick Gonsouland," interjected Andrew.

"You mean Alvarez Frederick Gonsouland," said Freddy in a

voice that was quite distinctive, "man of the world."

Andrew sat up in his seat, his voice a bit louder.

"Patricia Godbolt, Louis Cousins, Johnnie Rouse," he said. "What kinda colored names are dose? And Betty Jean Reed, dat's definitely a white girl's name."

"Whoa there, big guy," said Freddy, suddenly louder than Andrew. "Wouldn't matter what kinda name Betty Jean had, cause she got your nose open a mile wide."

"Man, don't talk so loud," said Andrew in a panicked whisper.

"Why, you scared to let her know you like her?"

Freddy cupped his hands to his mouth like a bullhorn.

"Hey, Betty Jean," he bellowed as Andrew pulled furiously on his arm. "Miss Betty Jean Reed!"

"Stop Man," said Andrew, "Don't start no trouble."

Too late, Betty Jean turned around to see Freddy, waving and smiling, trying to hoist up his buddy, Andrew, busily slinking in embarrassment.

"What is it, Freddy?" she said in that soft and tender voice.

"I need to tell you that my man, Andrew Heidelberg, thinks you are extremely attractive."

"Freddy," Andrew mumbled while giving a helpless and somewhat pained smile.

"You tell Mr. Andrew Heidelberg," said Betty Jean, "that I think he's extremely cute."

"I shall do that," boomed Freddy.

Sitting next to Betty Jean, Johnnie Rouse now decided that she had something to share with the entire bus.

"Girl," she said with a glare, "why you even wanna talk to Andrew? He's just a little freshman."

Betty Jean was not listening as she smiled at both Freddy and Andrew, then turned around to her giggling and meddlesome friends.

"Hey Andrew," said Freddy, "Betty Jean told me to tell you that you are really cute."

Andrew was still stunned.

"The girl must be blind," continued Freddy. "She probably just heard that you're a football player, and she likes those running backs. Of course, with you under that helmet, she can't see that ugly face. Yes, that's gotta be it."

Finally, realizing that Betty Jean had just given the sign that she thought he was handsome, Andrew sat back to brag.

"Hey, man," he said, "I'm smooth with da women and fast on da field."

"Yeah, you're Mr. Touchdown, all right," said Freddy. "Except you better get used to the fact that you won't be playing any football at Norview."

Andrew's mind quickly veered from Betty Jean to his favorite sport.

"That's what da white folks sayin now, but once dey see how good we are, dey gon beg us to play on da team," said Andrew. "I sure would like to be runnin in those beautiful Norview uniforms. Freddy, man, dey got some sweet uniforms. You know dey bad cause dey state champs."

"Well, they're the white state champs," said Freddy, "so you can forget about your black butt in those fancy uniforms. They sure ain't gonna have no Negroes on their team. They don't even want us in their school."

"Yeah, but I can dream," said Andrew.

"Man, you do a lotta dreaming," said Freddy, returning his stare out the window to the New Jersey countryside.

Dream he did ... Betty Jean Reed, a love that would last forever. Later that evening, Andrew and Betty Jean sat next to each other at a stage show in Atlantic City, watching Bobby Darin perform his hits—*Splish Splash, Queen of the Hop, Dream*

Lover ... and some new songs, *Mack the Knife* and *Beyond the Sea*.

With every note, Andrew fell deeper in love. After the concert, he and Betty Jean broke away from the crowd, finally alone on the top landing at the Diving Horse Show. Looking down from the semi-circled, wooden, wall-like structure jutting out into the Atlantic, they quietly watched a horse fall through the air and splash into the ocean. Andrew kept trying to think of something cool or intelligent to say, but the more his mind pressed, the more he tumbled into a silent vacuum.

"Hey, Andrew Heidelberg," Betty Jean said in her wondrous voice. "How come for a boy who talks so much, you suddenly are out of words?"

Andrew took a deep breath.

"Maybe cause I, uh, sorta, get quiet around ..."

Andrew paused. It was time to be bold.

"I just have a hard time," he said, "talkin to such a pretty girl."

Betty Jean smiled and moved ever so close with a soft kiss on his lips. He was stunned.

"Andrew Heidelberg, you think I'm pretty?"

"Yeah, real pretty," said Andrew with a sound half-filled with air.

Betty Jean put her hand into Andrew's hand and rested her head on his arm. Andrew took a deep breath, glanced down at her shining black hair, then gazed up to the star-filled sky. Once again, he lost all concept of speech.

****

Andrew and Bobby were walking on the side of Sewell's Point Road.

"How yo tutorin school goin, Bird?" asked Bobby.

"Good, man ... her name is Betty Jean Reed," said Andrew, as if that explained his entire life.

"Oooh," said Bobby, immediately realizing his best friend was hopelessly in love.

"Oh yeah, man," said Andrew. "She from Titustown, and she fine, and she already 15 years old. She don care how old I am, she like me anyway. Man, oh man, is she pretty."

Bobby wondered if Andrew had the maturity to handle an older woman.

"She's a whole year older den you?" he asked.

"She in the tenth grade," said Andrew. "And she goin to Granby."

"Oh Lord," said Bobby, "I guess we gon be goin way out to Titustown now, huh? What she look like again?"

Andrew looked to the heavens and smiled.

"She sho is fine," he said, shaking his head from side to side. "Umph, umph, umph ..."

Still staring at the sky and thinking about Betty Jean, Andrew began to wander onto the road.

"Damn, Bird," said Bobby as he grabbed Andrew's shirt and pulled him to safety. "You in love?"

"I must be, Knuck."

"Man, you is one lost soul," said Bobby, shaking his head.

****

Really, Andrew had plenty to keep his mind reasonably focused away from his obsession for Betty Jean. The Crusaders had crushed their first three opponents. Andrew, having been moved from quarterback to halfback, led the league in touchdowns. That was the good news.

The other side of his life occurred each morning as he

watched most of his friends board the bus for the eight-mile trip across the city to Booker T. Washington High School. He would take the next VTC bus that would travel through downtown Norfolk, dropping him within walking distance of the Bute Street Church. It had only been two weeks, but tutoring school was already becoming tedious. The teachers were young, brilliant, and dynamic. They were also extremely demanding. Homework took hours and Andrew had to study late into the night just to keep pace. He had always prided himself on being intelligent, but this was ridiculous. Perhaps, too, the attention and notoriety of the entire desegregation debacle had ever so subtly begun to wear thin on his psyche. It was all too difficult—barely enough time to play football, and just a trace of time left over for being in love.

At the end of one long day, Andrew and his brother were in their bedroom, the radio blasting *Don't Let Go* by Roy Hamilton. Andrew was reading the *Virginian-Pilot'* sports page and unconsciously singing along to the refrain.

"Don't let go ... don't let ..."

"Hey Kenny," said Andrew. "Says here this guy Eddie Versprille, number 21 for Norview, is the best halfback in da state, and they already 2-0. Crazy stuff. We were talkin bout dat in tutorin school. Dem white kids ain't goin ta school, but dey playin football."

"Yep," said Kenny, continuing to read his textbook.

The song ended and the radio cruised into something about "news at the top of the hour." Andrew was hardly listening, his focus having returned to the all-white sports pages that, as usual, had absolutely nothing about any Colored athletes. But processing bits and pieces, both boys were suddenly drawn full force back to the radio, something being reported about Governor Almond releasing an executive order to officially shut down six white public schools in Norfolk.

"Affecting more than 9,900 children," the newscaster was saying, "Norfolk becomes the largest school closing in United States history. And, in related news, a group of Negroes known as the Norfolk 17 ..."

Andrew sat straight up in his bed.

"... continue to be privately tutored at a local church with the known assistance of the NAACP."

And that was it. Something else about segregationists in the Tidewater area applauding the school closures and then some white lady started blaming the entire problem on *The Negroes*. Her son should have been a senior at Maury High School but would rather not graduate. She said proudly that her son was willing to make that sacrifice to keep the schools safe and segregated.

Andrew clenched his teeth, as if the racist woman's cracker kid was some sort of hero. Finally, the interview concluded, and the newscaster came back on air, talking about several groups separately contesting the shutdowns by suing the school board.

"And from Washington," the newscaster added. "President Eisenhower today condemned the school closures, reminding Governor Almond that the U.S. military is integrated and that the high number of service families in the Tidewater area will be adversely affected."

This was getting complicated, realized Andrew, although it was easy to separate the good guys from the bad ones. The radio now played a tape of Governor Almond, from his mansion in Richmond, firing back at the President of the United States as if what goes on in Virginia wasn't any of his business. The governor was furious at President Eisenhower.

"These civil rights programs that oppose massive resistance are ribald, unconstitutional, politically designed, cheap and tawdry," roared the Virginia governor. "They are communistically conceived and sponsored. We will never surrender to the mixing of the races, even when it appears that the Supreme Court wants to make it lawful for a Negro to intermarry with a white person."

Now, there was an idea foreign to Andrew's mind. Intermarry with a white person? What kind of idiot with a death wish would want to do that?

Chapter 7
Hazards of Smoking

Practice was over and, as always, Coach Becoate was impatiently attempting to gather his team. Most of the players began to huddle around the popular coach but paying attention to him was not particularly a team strength. The chatter continued about school or girls or whatever momentarily blazed through their minds. Andrew's voice, as usual, was the loudest.

"Listen up, guys," boomed Becoate, raising both arms to stress silence. "Boys, quiet, shut up for a minute. Heidelberg, the real coach is talking."

That got the attention as nearly everyone joined the coach in jovially telling Andrew to be quiet. They laughed and gathered nearer to the coach, finally listening, ultimately hoping he might blast Andrew again.

"Okay, knock it off," said Becoate. "Everybody take a knee."

Finally, everyone was quiet, gathering in a rather flexible circle, each resting on a knee. Immediately, Bobby raised his hand.

"Coach, I got a question."

"What is it, Bobby?"

Bobby stood and pointed at Andrew.

"Hey, Coach, after practice, can we lynch dis white boy?"

Amid great laughter, Andrew jumped up and playfully tried to grab Bobby in a bear hug from behind.

"Let's kill da white boy now," yelled one of the other players, as if giving the signal for an all-out attack, the players laughing wildly as they jumped on Andrew and pretended to pound him into submission, their victim delighting in the attention.

"Okay, okay fellas, knock it off," interjected Becoate, trying to portray seriousness and laugh at the same time. "C'mon, settle down. This is important."

Again, he had commanded their focus. Talk fast, he told himself.

"Lot of you guys think you must be the greatest football players in history because we got a 6-0 record," he continued. "And you're out there bragging because we haven't given up a single point all year. Every one of you think that nobody is ever gonna score against us. And then you laugh at the Bulldogs like they ain't got no chance cause they're in last place. Well, ya'll better wake up right now and stop with the lip. Ya'll can brag when the game is over. Understand?"

"Yes sir," came the group reply, most wishing tomorrow's game was already here.

"One other thing," said the coach. "I heard that some of you guys been seen behind the bleachers smoking cigarettes. I don't think I need to remind you about the rules."

The boys all looked around at their teammates, a few appearing guilty out of habit, but all realizing that rules only really mattered when caught by an adult. Still, this was a good time to offer up the names of teammates who had undoubtedly crossed the line of underage smoking.

"I'm not saying who it is," said Becoate, trying to ignore the barrage of possible suspects being so easily given up by friends.

"I'm saying that athletes don't smoke."

"Scuse me, Coach," interrupted Andrew while turning to Bobby. "Hey Knuck, let me have one of doze Winston's in yo bag over dere."

Once again laughter erupted, this time Bobby at the center of the siege.

"Yeah, Knuck, gimme a smoke," said another player.

"Fellas, you heard what I said," grumbled the coach. "If I catch you smoking, you ain't gonna be playing. See ya'll tomorrow."

With dusk fast approaching, the group began to separate, heading in all directions, enjoying the seemingly perfect life. Grabbing their jackets, Bobby and Andrew walked slowly from the big field beside Oakwood Elementary School toward Sewell's Point Road.

"So, Bird," said Bobby, "tell the truth. What in da hell y'all be doin in dat damn school in da basement?"

"What da hell you think we be doing in school? Man, we be workin ow ass off. I might as well be in college. Dis lady, Miss Perry da principal, she always on our case and, man, I never seen nobody so old. She graduated from Harr-varrd. An she sho loves to say Harr-varrd."

"Say what?" said Bobby, trying to figure out what exactly his friend was talking about.

"You know," said Andrew, "she from Harr-varrd University."

Bobby was still blank.

"Where da heck is Harr-varrd?"

"Way up North, man, in Boss-tonn," said Bird. "Don't worry, Knuck, you ain't goin der."

Bobby laughed in agreement, then mimicked his friend.

"So is Harr-varrd, harrrd?"

"Ya damn skippy it's hard," said Andrew. "And so is da damn tutorin school. Man, we do a ton a work erre day and lotsa homework erre night. It's crazy, man."

"So, hi yo girlfriend, Betty Jean?"

"Oh, she still fine. She real fine."

Reminded of his love, Andrew began to sing and dance to his well-rehearsed version of the Fiestas great hit.

"So fine, so fine, my baby so doggone fine ..."

Andrew momentarily abandoned the melody to add a unique and slick dance step, then quickly warbled another few lines.

"She send cold chills up and down my spine ... whoa-ho-wo-wo, whoa-ho-wo-wo, so fine."

As the boys walked and Andrew dreamed out loud, Bobby pulled a pack of Winston cigarettes out of his jacket and methodically put one in his mouth.

"Whatchu doin, fool?" said Andrew. "It wont five minutes ago Coach told us he better not catch us smokin."

Ignoring Andrew, Bobby lit the cigarette, took a deep puff, and casually blew smoke into the air.

"Save me a drag, Knuck," said Andrew.

"Nope, you don't smoke, member? Sides, Coach Beacote might see ya and set cho ass on da bench. Worse yet, da Colonel find out and yo nevva leave yo house again."

"Nigga, just save me a drag," said Andrew, grabbing Bobby's arm.

"Damn, man, don't have a nicotine fit," said Bobby, jerking away from his friend as he tried to laugh and puff at the same time. Finally, he passed the cigarette to Andrew, who savored the moment by taking a slow and long drag before returning the treasure to Bobby.

"Hey, Bird, are all da teachers old like dat Harrr-varrd lady?" said Bobby after taking another drag.

"Naw man, most of dem real young," said Andrew, feeling good from the relaxing taste of the cigarette. "Oh man, you should see da math teacher. She must be bout twenty sumpin. She fine, man, wit real long hair. I kinda like her."

"Yeah, man," said Bobby, "You like erre body dat's fine."

"Ain't nuttin wrong wit dat. She is bad, man, take my word, she bad. And we got dis real cool Spanish teacher, too."

"Yeah, I bet she fine, too, ain't she," said Bobby, taking his second puff in a row.

"It ain't no *she*, nigga, it's a *he*," said Andrew, shaking his head and looking closely at the burning cigarette. "Dr. Rodolfo Cejas, all da way from Cuba. Erre mornin he always say, 'Buenos dios, Andres. Como esta usted?' Man, he wears the baddest rags I ever seen. Real cool, I mean he cleaner than a mosquito's peter."

They both laughed as Andrew motioned for another smoke and Bobby playfully protected the cigarette before reluctantly handing it back to his best friend. But, just as Andrew inhaled and they rounded the corner of the house, someone stood staring them both in the face. It was Coach Beacote.

Andrew gulped, desperately trying to blow out the smoke as he fumbled, then dropped the cigarette, squashing the evidence with his shoe. Too late ...

"Looks to me like you're the one with the Winston's, Bird," said Becoate, "Guess you'll be the one at the end of the bench tomorrow."

As the coach turned and walked away, Andrew chased after him.

"Wait a minute, Coach. Hey, Coach, let me explain."

Becoate had already entered a friend's apartment, closing the door before Andrew could finish his plea.

Andrew stared helplessly at the door, but the coach did not return. This was not fair.

Bobby looked seriously at Andrew as though offering important advice.

"Bird, I think y'otta stop smokin, man," he said. "Dat shit ain't good fo yo health."

****

Coach Becoate was stunned. How could this be possible? The Bulldogs were easily the worst team in the league. This should be no contest. But now, only one quarter left, and the game was scoreless. Beacote gritted his teeth and walked past Andrew, trying to ignore his star running back sitting on the bench, smug as ever. This was not good. With Heidelberg in the game, Beacote knew the Crusaders would be running away with this one. But, where were his other so-called stars? The team showed no energy, no desire.

Damn cigarettes. He needed to forget the punishment and get Andrew back into the game. But what kind of example would that be? Then again, he only said he would sit him on the bench, he didn't say for how long.

Andrew watched his coach pacing back and forth, frustration mixed with anger. Of course, Andrew was also angry. They weren't even his cigarettes. Knuck should be sitting on the bench, not him. Who made up that stupid rule, anyway? Andrew watched the clumsy Bulldogs, the lethargic Crusaders.

"C'mon guys, get it goin," he yelled with 11 minutes left, Crusaders first and long from their own 15 after a holding penalty.

Andrew could only watch the destruction of a perfect season, realizing a certain sense of satisfaction that, without him, the team had not scored. Arrogance? No, just a harsh reality.

Becoate looked at Andrew, again. It was second-and-13 with the clock winding down. Certainly, the Bulldogs could not score against the mighty Crusader defense. But even the improbable was possible. A sense of panic swept through Becoate's withered mind as he pictured the embarrassment of facing his friends at work. Wouldn't matter if it was a loss or tie, the humiliation could never be erased. He looked again at the field, his pathetic team near panic and the stupid Bulldogs thinking they were the New York Giants.

"C'mon guys, where's the effort?" he yelled.

He looked down in disgust.

"Damn," he said to himself, then looked quickly to his star running back. Punishment over.

"Heidelberg," he yelled, "Get in there."

"Yes sir," said Andrew in a told-you-so voice as he grabbed his helmet, then sprinted into the game, not even asking if there was a certain play the coach cared to call.

Approaching the huddle, Andrew was greeted with the enthusiasm reserved for a savior. The spark was immediate. Pitch right and Andrew streaked past the Bulldogs as if they need not even bother to chase, 83 yards untouched to paydirt.

The rest happened so quickly that even Andrew was surprised at how much he meant to the team. Four carries, four touchdowns and the Crusaders had a 28-0 victory over the shell-shocked Bulldogs.

As the teams shook hands and the Crusaders celebrated on the sidelines, Coach Becoate approached Andrew.

"Nice job, Bird," he said. "I hope you learned a lesson from all of this tonight."

"Yes sir," answered Andrew with a beaming smile, "I sho did, Coach."

Becoate put up his hand to make a point and underscore that this had been his plan all along.

"Good," he said, "don't let it happen again."

The coach turned and began to walk away. All was back on course.

"Hey, Coach," said Andrew.

Beacote turned around, half expecting an apology.

"I learned two things tonight, Coach," said Andrew.

"What was that, Bird?"

Andrew spoke slowly, with flawless pronunciation.

"First, I learned that athletes definitely should not smoke," he said.

"That's right, Bird," said the coach. "You remember that."

Nodding his head in silent victory, Andrew paused until he had the complete attention of his coach. Andrew gave a sly smile.

"An, Coach, da second thing I learned is ... if ya wanna win da game, gimme da ball."

It was never easy for Andrew Heidelberg to be humble.

Chapter 8

Yet Another Famous Smoker

Usually a study in charm and composure, Mrs. Mason was as excited as a giddy teenager as she stood before the 17 youngsters in the church basement. Andrew had already been through several of these assemblies, but this seemed urgent. Obviously, the tutoring school was not about to be attacked by Senator Byrd and the Ku Klux Klan ... Mrs. Mason seemed way too thrilled. Perhaps all the racists in Virginia had agreed to move south of the North Carolina border? Or maybe everyone was going back to Atlantic City so Andrew could spend the entire weekend with Betty Jean? Whatever, Andrew was getting excited by the commotion.

"Good morning, scholars," said Mrs. Mason. "Please give me your attention. I have just received some very exciting news."

She paused as the entire room, including teachers, anxiously stared.

"Next week," she continued, "Edward R. Murrow, the famous commentator of the CBS television shows, *See it Now* and *Person to Person*, will broadcast a special presentation from right here in Bute Street Baptist Church. It will be seen across the entire nation. You all are really going to be famous now."

68

Andrew poked Freddy, then quickly caught Betty Jean's eyes. She was beautiful, excited. This was very cool. One of the most famous people in America was coming to Norfolk.

"Television, man," Andrew jabbered at Freddy while smiling at his girlfriend.

Andrew pulled back, realizing Mrs. Mason was giving him her *shush* stare.

"Mr. Murrow plans to broadcast this particular show relative to Virginia's massive resistance movement and the school lockouts," she continued, politely smiling as Andrew returned to listening. "The NAACP is obviously thrilled that he will be coming to our school. I think that this national notoriety indicates the importance and magnitude of what you scholars are doing and how much the entire world is watching your performance."

Betty Jean raised her hand.

"Yes, Betty Jean," said Mrs. Mason, still glowing.

"Is Mr. Murrow going to ask us any individual questions?"

"I would expect he might interview some of you," said Mrs. Mason.

Without waiting to be recognized or thinking beyond the obvious, Andrew stood to address the room, bursting into the conversation with clear, precise English.

"I would welcome the opportunity," Andrew said in a deep, rich voice, "to speak to the national audience."

While most of the students snickered in fun, Johnnie Rouse was evidently not amused.

"Andrew, you are such an idiot," she said.

"Amen to that," giggled Freddy.

****

Heidelberg

Andrew already knew that Edward R. Murrow was known across the world and had even seen him on TV a few times. He was always struck by Murrow's powerful and raspy voice, but not really interested in what he might be saying since it was always part of some news broadcast.

But there he was, Edward R. Murrow, in the basement of the Bute Street Baptist Church, talking directly to Mrs. Mason as if she were white or something.

The place was a zoo of motion as white men set up cameras and lights, several other white men writing down thoughts.

What struck Andrew about Murrow were his eyes, darting around the room as if looking for something he might have lost. The man was obviously smart, no doubt spent a lot of time thinking.

Andrew had never really looked at a white man up close. Usually, he diverted his eyes—best to act disinterested, safest to take a different path ... that, or just run like hell.

But, today, Andrew felt a streak of bravery as he closely watched the white television god light up another Camel cigarette, right there in the Baptist Church. Edward R. Murrow was at least 50 years old, tall and thin with a weathered and somewhat disturbing face. His eyes were penetratingly dark and seemingly explosive, a man in charge ... and probably not too patient. Damn, thought Andrew, Edward R. Murrow had the look of a white racist, except he wasn't, not by the way he was chatting with Mrs. Mason. And not by the look on her face to be in the presence of someone so important.

Chapter 9
All Things Change

*L*ate January and Andrew desperately needed a break from the constant push of school. The pressure of unrelenting study had perhaps strengthened his brain, but it had worn thin on his nerves. Projects, tests, homework. If life were football, Andrew would have nothing left but pride and stubbornness.

Okay, Edward R. Murrow had put the Norfolk 17 on national television, and they had even been featured in *Life Magazine*. But the walls of the tutoring school were beginning to close in on Andrew. He struggled, worked, and struggled some more.

The world would quickly change.

On Monday, January 19, 1959, in two landmark decisions, both the Virginia Supreme Court and federal court in Norfolk had ruled that schools must be opened and integrated. Not only were the closings a violation of the Virginia Constitution, but they also violated the 14th amendment of the United States Constitution. Of course, none of that seemed to matter to the likes of Senator Byrd or Governor Almond.

"We will oppose with every ounce of our energy the attempt being made to mix the white and Negro races in our classrooms," said Governor Almond in his eloquent, white southern politician drawl. "Let there be no misunderstanding, no weasel words on this point: we dedicate our every capacity to preserve segregation in our schools."

But that had been last week. On Monday evening, the 26th of January, Andrew was studying Spanish at the kitchen table when the news broke on the radio.

"A dramatic turnaround today in Richmond," the newscaster reported. "Exactly one week after vowing that he would forever fight against integration in public schools, Governor Lindsay Almond told the legislature, 'We cannot secede, and we cannot reverse the Supreme Court of the United States.' Saying that the majority of the white people in Virginia want the schools to re-open, Governor Almond stated that resistance at this point would only empower the NAACP to control the degree and tempo of integration. The Governor said he believes Virginia will show the world a dignified and orderly transition to integration."

"We'll see," said Andrew's mother, certainly wanting to dance and sing, yet knowing from experience it was far too early to celebrate.

The next morning at tutoring school, Andrew figured the hastily called assembly undoubtedly had something to do with the governor's concession. Then again, perhaps old Senator Byrd had come up with another way to keep the schools white.

Mrs. Mason and Mrs. Perry were both smiling as the 17 students and their teachers gathered in the main basement room.

"Students, I have important news," said Mrs. Perry. "The state has ordered the public schools to reopen next Monday, February 2. We will only have four more days of tutoring school. It seems strange that something we've been battling for so long is now happening so fast."

It took a moment for her words to take hold. But, like a fire in a dry forest, there was no denying reality, even if the excitement was tempered with apprehension.

Still, there was Mrs. Perry standing up there in front of this small world, wiping tears from her eyes as if this might really be true. Mrs. Mason, with a huge smile of victory, put her hand on Mrs. Perry's shoulder.

"I want to thank Mrs. Perry and all the teachers who have so graciously volunteered their time for your education," said Mrs. Mason, pausing to wipe her own tears. "Never forget that the NAACP, and all of us in this room, will be with you in spirit and always available to help."

Later that day, Andrew found a moment alone with his girlfriend.

"Betty Jean," he said quietly, "I think I'm gonna miss this place."

****

It was the last day of January, less than four days until Andrew would storm the walls of Norview High School. He was continually nervous, the nagging thought of doom refusing to leave him alone. How did he get into this mess? What if he were caught looking at a white girl? It was an accident, he would say, if they even let him speak before the hanging.

Bobby hit the black 8-ball smack into the side pocket.

"Oh yeah, whipped you again," he proclaimed.

Harry's Pool Room was nothing more than a large wood-framed, one-room cottage with bare white walls and four pool tables set in T-formation. Wooden benches lined the side walls. Harry, the owner, usually sat on a high stool located in the back of the room next to the table with the cash register.

Forever punctual, Harry had gone home for dinner 28 minutes earlier, having left Charlie, his long-time and only employee,

73

in charge. Although Charlie had little education, he did have a wonderful sense of humor. On this particular evening, with Harry due to return in precisely two minutes, Charlie was deviously changing the radio station, finally settling on the pure white sounds of *Come Softly to Me* by The Fleetwoods.

Several of the older men groused at Charlie's choice of music, but he assured them it was only for a moment.

"Les jes see what happens," Charlie whispered with a grin, not having to wait long for Harry to walk through the door at his usual time, struck with a sudden look of horror.

"Who da hell been messin wit da radio?" he boomed, immediately glaring at Charlie while the regulars futilely attempted to hide their laughter.

Charlie, who walked with a noticeable limp, quickly vacated Harry's high seat as the owner stormed toward his radio. Charlie slapped the back of Harry's shoulder while sliding a rack along the table as the environment became overtaken by complete hilarity.

"It ain't funny, Charlie," grumbled Harry, who immediately fiddled with the dial to locate his station, thankfully finding Dinah Washington's *What a Difference a Day Makes*. Harry turned up the volume.

"Oh, dat's da sound," he said, his demeanor suddenly calm and introspective. "Sing it, Dinah."

Playing at the next table, Andrew and Bobby were hardly paying attention to the older men. With the look of genius, Bobby again buried the 8-ball.

"Damn," blurted Andrew, who had just finished complaining that his last shot had only missed because the table was crooked.

Of course, a major problem at Harry's Pool Room was that the room itself leaned ever so slightly, a definite disadvantage to rookies or strangers. Andrew was having trouble with far more than the slant.

"Hey Bird, seem like yo game is weak as skim piss today," gloated Bobby. "You must be gettin da heebie-geebies thinkin bout goin up dere wit all dem white people."

"You think dat shit funny, dontcha Knuck?" said Andrew flipping a quarter on the table to pay for the game as Charlie racked the balls.

Bobby paused from chalking his cue and looked seriously at Andrew.

"Naw, Bird, it ain't funny. It's crazy as hell you goin up dere wit dem crackers. Whachu think gon happen when dem white boys from Southern Shopping Center remember yo black butt?"

Knowing he had exposed the reason for his friend's gloom, Bobby added a theatrical impression.

"Hello, Mr. Cracker, um Andrew Heidelberg, your new classmate. You member me. I busted yo car window out last week wit one of my lucky rocks."

"I think I'll tell dem where you live, nigga," Andrew interrupted. "You hit more cars den me, Knuck."

"Bird, dey don't care who throwed da most rocks when dey got da rope round yo neck."

"I hope you ain't fine with dat," said Andrew, his voice searching for an apology.

Bobby picked up the anxiety and turned off the humor.

"Bird, now you know we family," he said softly. "I be prayin fo you."

****

Andrew was slowly walking home on the bank of Sewell's Point Road, preoccupied with thoughts of the upcoming week and reminding himself once again to never look at white girls, even the ugly ones. The cold, stark woods only intensified his gloom.

Suddenly, a car full of white teenagers, girls and boys, singing and laughing, drove past. On instinct, Andrew tensed, expecting a new dose of harassment. The kids in the car glanced at Andrew but continued down the road, seemingly lost inside their own peculiar worlds, as if he didn't exist.

Andrew's mind returned to deep thought, that his life could be ending soon, and he could not control the fall.

****

Andrew was sitting on his bed, sorting through a pile of papers and books from tutoring school, wondering if anything was worth saving.

Even though it was Sunday night, his brother had gone to the library at Norfolk State. No doubt Kenny Jr. would be studying with some girl.

As usual, Andrew had closed the bedroom door so he could turn up the radio. Still, whatever was playing, he was not paying attention. Instead, his eyes were focused on the disfigured remains of poor Emmett Till's head, smack in the middle of the September 1955 issue of *Jet Magazine*.

Andrew's mind began racing to the places he did not want to go. It only happened three years ago, he thought, and it seemed that Emmett had died a million times, each crushing blow only magnifying the massive mush that once was a kid's face.

In the movies, Andrew had seen people killed all the time, a bullet hole to the chest they politely covered before tumbling to the soft ground. That was how people were supposed to die, not like Emmett Till.

A knock on the bedroom door broke Andrew's runaway panic,

the voice of his mother sending the old magazine flying under the bed, his hand quickly grabbing a history paper from school.

"Well, my son, you're very quiet this evening," Mrs. Heidelberg said as she entered the room and sat down beside him, a comforting smile mixed with a soothing voice. "Getting a little nervous about your big day tomorrow?"

"Um sho glad you can smile," said Andrew while lowering his head in dramatic sadness. "Cause I don't see nothin to make me happy."

As his mom put her hand around his shoulder and tried to gently pull him toward her, Andrew initially attempted to evade her warmth, but realized he had no escape, and could only sigh as she gave him a long and loving embrace. Finally, after what seemed to be an uncomfortable amount of time, Andrew's father entered the room to break the affection.

"Are you ready for your new school, Andrewkie?" said Mr. Heidelberg as he extended an open hand to rub his son's head.

"Um glad to be gitten outta dat tutoring school, I can tell you dat," said Andrew, finally able to breathe after being nearly suffocated by his loving mother. "But going to Norview and facing all dem white people dat I know gon wanna lynch me, I'on know bout dat."

"Boy, you ain't got nothing to be worrying about," said his father. "Ain't nobody gonna be lynching nobody. Do you really think we would send you up there if we thought somebody would hurt you?"

"Well, I can tell you I ain't talkin to no white girls," said Andrew. "I'on care how many speak to me."

Mrs. Heidelberg looked seriously into Andrew's eyes.

"Are you really scared?" she said.

"I ain't outta-my-mind scared," said Andrew, "but I like the way y'all gon be a hundred miles away and tellin me not to worry. I know by da time daddy git to me from da naval base, I'll already be dead."

"Andrew, stop being foolish," she said, her soft tone now leaning toward a touch of agitation. "You been around white people before. If you mind your own business, you'll be fine."

Andrew looked blankly at his mom. He had run out of arguments.

"So, are you walking to Norview by yourself tomorrow," she continued, "or are you going with Freddy?"

"Um gon meet Freddy over his house bout 8:30. We don't wanna be late, but we sho don't wanna be dere too early. Boy, what a sad, sad story. He was only 15 years old."

"Trust your mother, son, it'll all work out for the best. And, anyway, you have come too far to quit now. Just put your mind at ease. We'll see you in the morning."

As Andrew's parents left the room, shutting the door behind them, he gathered the tutoring school papers and books, pushing them under his bed. He turned off the light, wondering how much noise his brother would make when he got home from studying. He also started thinking about Betty Jean and how awful it was for her to be the only Black kid going to Granby. Two others would also be alone—Louis Cousins at Maury and Geraldine Talley at Northside Junior High. They *had* to be scared.

Andrew prayed, hoping for rest, but figuring he was far too anxious to sleep ...

****

In a dream, Andrew stood in a near-empty field, talking quietly to a disfigured Emmett Till.

"Emmett, you shoulda never left Chicago," Andrew said to his best friend.

"I hate Mississippi, Bird," said Emmett, his face horribly broken. "I think they gouged out my eye ... and my face is all messed up ... this bullet in my head sho hurts."

Suddenly, Andrew realized that he was now surrounded by a group of white men wearing sheets without hoods.

"Sorry, Bird," said Emmett, "um dead again ... cain't help ya now."

As the white men moved closer, Emmett fell back to the ground to once again die. Andrew looked up to now see what appeared to be hundreds of angry white men, armed with guns, baseball bats, and steel tools.

"Should we beat dat nigger with the hammers or just shoot him between the eyes?" said one of the men.

"Nah, let's make him bleed," said another.

Andrew noticed that the mob of white people also included women and children. They all seemed to be both incensed and excitedly happy at the same time. A young white girl moved in for a closer look.

"Look y'all, he's got his eyes all over me," said the girl, who was maybe 13 years old.

Andrew quickly looked away from her, but only to see a rope being thrown over the branch of a lone tree.

"Let's just hang the nigger," said another man.

The mob heartily agreed.

"Where's our hoods?" asked a man in a rather anxious voice. "We need our hoods."

A man stepped forward with a large cart of neatly folded white hoods.

"Fresh from the cleaners," he said.

The white people all started to grab for the hoods and quickly put them over their heads. But someone had forgotten to put holes for the eyes and none of the white people could see, each fidgeting to find the right adjustment. Instinctively, Andrew darted through a small opening between the blinded white bigots. The field was now wide open, but the only place to hide was the tree with the rope hanging from it. Andrew swiftly climbed up several branches, hiding just above the rope. The white people had now torn holes in their hoods, ready for the kill.

"Where'd dat black boy go?" said the young girl.

As the white people crashed into each other, they became more and more furious. But no one thought to look up where Andrew was hiding.

"He's gotta be near," said one of the men. "Let's spread out and search."

Everyone left. It was quiet. Andrew sat alone in the tree, unable to move. Suddenly, he felt a poke and was startled to see the young white girl in the branch next to him.

"Hi," she said.

****

Andrew sat straight up in his bed—sweating, scared, shaking ... awake.

Chapter 10

February 2, 1959

*I*t was early Monday morning, a blotch of gray light illuminating the old brown window shade. As always, the door opened.

"Andrew, oh Andrew, it's time to make your mark on the world," Mrs. Heidelberg chirped in a voice that was half-song, half-torture.

Andrew did not want to hear or move, hoping she would give up and walk away. She didn't. Now, she was shaking the top of his blanket.

"Come on son, breakfast is ready, and I know you don't wanna be late on your first day of school."

"No," Andrew muttered from beneath his covers.

"Kenny, you get up too, son," said Mrs. Heidelberg. "Just because you in college don't mean you can sleep all day."

Kenny moaned but did not stir.

Andrew lifted his head, stunned by the light from the window. But, as his mother left the room, he pulled the covers back over his head and collapsed beneath them.

Kenny had still not moved. Wait, wasn't this the day of his little brother's doom? Kenny jumped from his bed, bolted across the room, and yanked away Andrew's covers.

"C'mon, boy, you gotta whole lotta white people to see today," barked Kenny, far too excited.

Andrew tried to retrieve his blanket, but Kenny was determined to enjoy as much suffering as possible.

"Get up, boy," he ordered, pulling the last cover to the floor. "You cain't hide today!"

****

Dressed for school, Andrew sat down at the kitchen table to have a bowl of cereal with his father and brother.

"Man, dat was a weird night," he said.

"You were just anxious for your big day," answered Mr. Heidelberg, looking up at his wife with a proud smile.

"Lena, girl," he said, "your son is going to make a little history today."

Kenny interrupted, "And we sure hope he makes it back, cause ..."

"Boy, be quiet," Mrs. Heidelberg snapped, "we don't need no mess this morning. I didn't get you up first for you to sit around and bother your brother. I think Norfolk State is waiting for you."

"Yes ma'am, I'm leaving," said Kenny as he got up to rinse his bowl and place it in the drainboard.

"As I was saying, Andrew," continued his father, "this is a big day for the Heidelberg family and to show you how big, I've got my leather and corduroy jacket here specially for you. Wear it so you can look real good when the cameras start rolling. Never let it be said that a Heidelberg didn't look his best for the camera."

Andrew acted as if he was not that impressed, offering only a halfhearted smile.

"Thanks, Daddy," he said, "I'm sure your leather coat will look real good on me while I'm layin in my casket."

Mrs. Heidelberg immediately jumped into the conversation.

"Andrew, I told you and your brother to stop talking that foolish mess. Ain't nobody gonna put a finger on you."

"And, Boy, I'll tell you again," added his father. "If I even thought anybody was gon do something to you, I'd go with you myself. You just remember that the Lord is with you, so you are always safe. God is on your side."

Just as Mr. Heidelberg raised his finger to say more, a car horn from out front broke his thought. Instead, he jumped up, grabbed his lunch from the table, and put on his coat.

"That's my ride," he said. "Gotta go, Lena. God bless you, Son."

Kenny followed close behind his dad but paused at the front door to look at his brother.

"See ya later, white boy," he said. "And I wanna full report."

Putting on her coat, Mrs. Heidelberg shushed Kenny out the door and gave Andrew a dollar in change from her pocketbook.

"I'll see you this evening, Andrew," she said while leaning down to kiss him on the cheek. "Don't forget to lock my door."

Andrew put on his father's leather coat, took a deep breath, and opened the door, surprised to see Freddy about to knock. They exchanged greetings as Andrew stepped into the cold outside world, closed the door, and checked the lock.

****

To get to Norview, Andrew and Freddy agreed it would be safest to bypass Sewells Point Road for Chesapeake Boulevard. It was a wider path and separated from the two-lane road by huge ditches on either side. The sky was gloomy and the temperature chilly, maybe 40 degrees, as the boys skirted the edge of the thick woods that partially hid the small houses and bungalows of Oakwood and Rosemont.

Both were silent until they hit the path that would stretch all the way to the high school.

"Man, it's quiet this way," said Andrew, his jaw rather tight, his nerves a bit frazzled. "I thought there'd be a lotta white kids comin down from Ocean View, didn't you?"

"Naw, they usually go down Sewells Point," said Freddy, seemingly calm and confident. "I think they're afraid of the woods."

"Good," said Andrew, "cause I don't need to see none of them til I have to."

Andrew waited for a response from Freddy, but the older boy walked as if this were just another day. Andrew looked seriously at his friend.

"Are you scared, man?"

"No," answered Freddy.

"I'on know, man," said Andrew, "Norview got about 2,500 students. And all but eight of dem are white. Whatchou gon do if somebody tries to hit you, or spit on you?"

"Don't know," said Freddy, still nonchalant. "What are you gonna do?"

"Well, dey say we ain't spose to say nothin or do nothin if dey call us names and stuff. I ain't got no problem wit dat too much. But I ain't sayin I ain't gon do something if somebody be tryin to kill me. Um definitely gon be fightin back. I'on care what da NAACP say."

Freddy looked at Andrew, still acting unfazed.

"That's a nice jacket you got there," said Freddy, reaching over to rub the fabric.

"Dat's real leather, man," said Andrew. "My daddy hooked me up dis mornin."

Freddy grabbed Andrew's shoulder and looked closely at his face.

"You hot, man?"

"Naw, man, it's kinda cold out here," said Andrew, somewhat bewildered by the question. "Why?"

"Because you sure are sweating a lot on your nose," said Freddy.

Andrew quickly tried to wipe the sweat from his face, as if that might provide the secret to calmness. It didn't. The boys were getting closer to the rear of the high school.

"I'on see nobody," said Andrew. "Think maybe dey canceled school again and forgot to tell us?"

"I doubt it," said Freddy.

****

Past a large seven-foot fence running along the backside of the school property, a giant smokestack jutted into the air. It was eerily quiet as Freddy and Andrew rounded the side of the huge, red brick building with still nobody in sight.

But then, they turned the corner and were suddenly in full view of seemingly thousands of white people ... boys and girls, men and women. There are policemen everywhere, some wearing long, knee-length boots with stiff hats and holstered guns.

"Over here," they heard someone shout, setting off a near stampede in their direction. Suddenly, news cameras flashed as hostile voices screamed a plethora of chaotic chatter, the most discernible word being "nigger." Staggered by the scene, both Andrew and Freddy wanted to stop, retreat, but the crowd quickly closed in on them. They kept walking, slower, their defenses on high alert.

Amidst the slurs and screams, a stupid cheer grew louder.

"Two, four, six, eight, we don't want to integrate," many chanted in poetic exhilaration. "Two, four, six, eight, we don't

85

want to integrate."

More noise ...

"Niggers go home," some were screaming. "Go back to Africa where you belong, you filthy coons."

Andrew was shocked—his mind disconnected, his legs weak, his body pulled apart, the verbal taunts like jagged rocks aimed directly for his head, few missing their mark.

For some strange reason, it seemed as if his anger and humiliation had managed to pull his mind outside his own body, as if he were watching his own death, certain it would be accompanied by fierce and unrelenting pain.

"Hey, tar baby, get your nigger ass outta here."

As they tried to move toward the front door, Andrew momentarily saw a group of white boys standing on the steps at the corner of the building. It seemed as if the group was moving toward them in unison.

Andrew glanced at the once-confident Freddy, obviously overwhelmed with trepidation, jaw tight, searching for a way to somehow escape the terror.

"Here come two more niggers," one of the white boys angrily screamed.

Chaotic insanity ...

The crowd moved closer, a smothering wrath surrounding them. From a distance, many were singing slurs to the tune of *Old MacDonald Had A Farm.*

"Here a nigger, there a nigger, everywhere a nigger, nigger ..."

The boys tried to move forward, though they wanted to pull back. Maybe another day, another time.

"Niggers, coons, spear-chuckers, spooks ..." The words attacked from all directions, pounding like incoming bombs, nowhere on earth to hide.

Cameras broke through the crowd, jostled and thrust into the faces of the two boys. Reporters were trying to yell questions, many drowned by the noise. The surge was so tight that Andrew could feel the heat from their breath, the spit from their mouths.

"*Virginian-Pilot,*" one reporter yelled. "Are you boys scared?"

"*Richmond Times-Dispatch,*" another said. "Has anybody hit you?"

Perhaps staying close to the cameras would provide safety, perhaps not.

"What are your names?" asked the first reporter.

Now three, maybe four reporters were talking simultaneously: "How do you feel about what's happening? Are you surprised by this reception? Was it worth it to leave your colored schools and come here? Are you gonna like it here? Do you think you'll make it through the day?"

Just as the NAACP had instructed them, both boys attempted to avoid contact, but the reporters and the mass of bigots were directly in their faces. Andrew and Freddy remained silent, the insults relentlessly hammering their humanity.

****

The school bell rang. As the crowd moved instinctively toward the large front doors of the building, reporters and cameramen continued to follow Andrew and Freddy. Into the halls, it was absolute bedlam with the pushing and shoving of students jamming shoulder-to-shoulder. Nearly everyone seemed focused on Andrew and Freddy, looks of disdain mixed with vulgarity and threats.

"Where we spose go now, Freddy?" asked Andrew, trying to speak over the noise.

"Sophomores go to the cafeteria," said Freddy, his eyes straight ahead. "I'm not sure, but I think you're supposed to go to the auditorium. Just follow all those crazy freshmen."

Without even a glance, Freddy had veered off into a hallway leading to the cafeteria. Andrew tried to take a deep breath, but even that seemed difficult as he continued down the long hallway with the loud and wild freshmen hollering at him. When he finally reached the end of the hallway, he saw the entrances to the auditorium. He took another deep breath, hoping the room might somehow offer a trace of sanity. No way.

As he walked through one of the two-door entrances, the newest sport in town—nigger calling—heightened into total mayhem. It seemed to be great fun for the white hecklers.

"Go home, nigger," they yelled. "Get out, you dirty spook. Go back to your nigger people."

Searching for a place to sit, Andrew continued down the aisle with a futile attempt to act like he didn't hear the vulgar side of hate. Mostly, his mind was trying to process the reason God would possibly want to do this to him. But even that thought was short-lived as the commotion came from every angle. Andrew's eyes focused on the group of teachers standing on the stage, a long row of tables behind them. He immediately headed toward the teachers for safety. But, as he continued down the aisle, he heard loud and boisterous singing that seemed to be originating from the ceiling. Glancing backward, he was stunned to see a balcony with a group of freshman boys hanging over the rail with their arms extended and singing the familiar melody of The Coasters hit song, Charlie Brown. The words had been changed.

"Fee, fee, fi, fi, fo, fo fum, I smell a nigger in the auditorium. Charlie Brown, Charlie Brown. He's a clown, that Charlie Brown. He's gonna get hung, just you wait and see ... why's that nigger in school with me?"

It seemed as if the entire ninth-grade class was becoming increasingly rowdy, the white kids laughing and singing. Even some of the teachers were smiling and tapping their feet. Moving as quickly as he could without touching anyone, Andrew managed to find a seat about five rows from the front.

Still in the eye of the storm, he silently looked straight ahead. But now, with great fanfare, everyone in his row got up and moved. Moments later, everyone in the row behind him did the same. And that was repeated by everyone sitting in the row in front of Andrew, leaving him the only person in three rows of seats.

Ultimately, the teachers managed to control the chaos, issued instructions, and began calling names to hand out class schedules. The noise muffled to a quiet chatter until the teachers reached the "H" section and Andrew's name was finally called. As he got up and walked to the auditorium stage for his paperwork, the volume immediately intensified, the heckling, applause, and vulgar performance of *Charlie Brown* once again at full blast.

"That nigger better not be in my class," someone yelled within the howls of the crowd.

****

With self-protection his primary thought, Andrew entered his homeroom class and quickly selected a front-row desk closest to the windows. If need be, he figured the window might prove his best path for escape.

The moment he sat down, the students at the desk next to him and behind both ceremoniously got up and moved. As the teacher wrote instructions on the blackboard, spit wads flew, aimed at the back of Andrew's head. A paper airplane also sailed past, just missing its target. When the teacher turned around, she acted as if she did not notice anything out of the ordinary.

Heidelberg

"Oh, no," said a white boy quite loudly. "Don't tell me we got a real live nigger in our homeroom. Ya'll better not get too close. You never know what diseases them niggers got."

Most of the students laughed, but Andrew looked straight ahead. The teacher, still acting oblivious to any disturbances, opened her attendance book.

"Good morning, students," she said, carefully keeping her eye contact away from Andrew. "I want to welcome you to the ninth grade. Please give me your undivided attention and answer when I call your name."

"Do niggers have names?" one of the boys asked in a loud whisper.

Above the continued laughter of students, the teacher called the roll.

****

Every class was the same—isolation and harassment, teachers deaf to the taunts. The halls were louder and more obtrusive. The danger felt overwhelming, protection nonexistent. He may as well have been trapped in an alien world.

Several girls were terrified that Andrew might get near or bump into them or somehow touch them. One dropped her books, gave a high-pitched scream, and ran down the hall hysterically.

Shrieks and laughter mixed with hatred and stares. Andrew was humiliated, angry, exhausted. This was beyond anything the NAACP had predicted.

****

A few minutes past 12:30, Andrew entered the school cafeteria, quite hungry from the morning's relentless trauma. He had never seen such a large cafeteria, a room at least twice as large as the eating areas of the colored junior high and high school combined.

Noisy chatter and laughter filled the cafeteria, but, like dominoes collapsing, there was suddenly a deafening silence as all eyes watched him enter. The eerie vacuum lasted about 10 seconds as Andrew walked to the serving line, his head down to avoid eye contact. As the noise again picked up, it was interspersed with names he'd heard all morning.

A photographer approached unexpectedly, the flashbulb of his camera momentarily blinding Andrew. Saying nothing, the man quickly moved to the side for another shot as Andrew approached the end of the long line moving toward the kitchen entrance. Andrew was careful to keep a safe distance from the other students, but his position at the end of the line put him in the middle of the cafeteria.

"Don't let that nigger touch your food," someone bellowed.

"Hi," said a soft and friendly voice from behind him.

Andrew turned slowly to see an attractive white girl, tall and slender with long dark hair. Andrew gulped. Don't talk to white girls, he thought. Immediately, the photographer stopped taking pictures and walked away.

"Hi, how are you?" he said with a nervous tone.

"Oh, I'm fine," she said with a smile. "It must be awfully hard on you with all this attention."

"Well, it's just a little nerve-racking," said Andrew, totally forgetting Rule #1.

"I apologize for how the kids are treating you," she said. "Some of us just need to grow up. I hope the day gets better for you."

"Thanks," said Andrew as he turned around to follow the line.

He noticed that teachers were seated at the last table before entering the food area. He would need to sit close to them.

Andrew turned to speak again to the attractive girl, but she was gone.

****

Andrew walked through the door into the serving area and was shocked by a clear and friendly voice from behind the food counter.

"Hello, Andrew Heidelberg."

Andrew's eyes locked onto a colored lady serving food, graced by a beautiful and proud smile. He beamed with recognition and a weird flood of excitement that nearly brought tears to his eyes.

"Hey, Miss Eddie Mae," he said. It felt so good to see someone he knew.

Andrew noticed the other Black workers were also proudly smiling.

"Andrew, how are you today?" one of the other women said.

"Um fine," he said. "I sure am glad to see y'all."

"Well, we sure are glad to see you too, Andrew Heidelberg," said Miss Eddie Mae, the mother of four of Andrew's good friends. "You go on, son. Everything will be fine."

Andrew saw a tall, colored man standing behind the counter drying a huge pot with his towel.

"Hi, son, you okay?" he said with a deep voice.

"Yes sir, thanks," Andrew said, nodding his head up and down as if he had somehow found a safe haven.

Andrew continued around the u-shaped area to an expressionless white cashier and paid for his meal.

****

Andrew stood, leaning against the wall near the teachers, waiting for a vacant seat at a table nearby.

His mind was jumbled, bouncing out of control in the cavity of his brain. He tried to focus on Miss Eddie Mae's smile, anything for comfort. He thought momentarily of the white girl who had talked to him, then disappeared. He realized that if he were to see her again, he would have no recognition whatsoever. What did she look like? His brain was too battered to function. And, damn, he had broken his main rule—don't look at or talk to any white girls. Everybody in the entire cafeteria was watching. He would never survive the day.

Finally, a student finished his lunch and got up from the table, Andrew quietly taking the empty seat. Such a bold act seemed a shock to the other students at the table, who all stopped eating to stare at him for several seconds, along with other students at other tables. The teachers, as had been the case all day, were obliviously ignoring the situation by continuing to eat and chatter.

It didn't take 15 seconds after Andrew had sat down that the boy next to him tossed his fork onto the table.

"My food is beginning to stink," he grumbled as he overturned his tray, looked disgustedly at Andrew, and left.

"Damn niggers," said another boy, who also got up and dramatically headed for the trashcan to the laughter of students at the adjacent tables.

The boy sitting across from Andrew immediately took a huge whiff, his face turning sour as his hands tried to fan away the imaginary smell.

"Damn, my food stinks too," he said as he got up to dump his lunch in the trash.

Now, everyone at the table was leaving, loudly complaining about the stench of their food.

"Smells like nigger food," announced the final white boy to stand. "I think I'm gonna be sick."

Andrew was once again humiliated as he sat alone, everyone staring, including the teachers. He looked at his food and tried to eat, then dabbled it several times with his fork. Finally, he stood to take his food to the trash.

"Umph, I think mine stinks too," he mumbled.

****

Andrew left the cafeteria as quickly as he could walk and headed down the somewhat secluded hallway to the gymnasium where his PE class was scheduled to start in about 15 minutes.

"Okay, Andrew," he said to himself, "keep it together. Just go to da gym class."

His mind broke to another direction.

"And they worried about me being sassy," he grumbled to himself. "I hate em all. If one of them even comes close to touchin me, I'll ... slow down, Andrew, remember what the NAACP said. Just keep cool."

At the end of the hall, near the entrance to the gym, Andrew noticed a distinct line of football team photos on the walls. The larger encased pictures were for the State Championship teams and the slightly smaller pictures were for the Eastern District championship teams. It was obvious that Norview had a long tradition of being a state football powerhouse because pictures were stretched along both sides of the walls around the gymnasium. As he viewed and studied the pictures, two students approached from behind.

"What are you looking at, nigger?" said one of the boys. "You ain't never gonna see no coons up there."

Both white boys laughed and continued down the hall.

94

Andrew stood alone, still looking at the photos, shaking his head in subdued anger.

****

After the final bell of the day, the last spit wad finding the back of his head, Andrew quickly left class and moved toward the front door of the school, suppressed by the blur of whites repeating the same slander and threats he had heard all day.

In front of the building, the students had stopped their exit to form stray pockets that furiously melded into a wild and angry crowd.

One white boy jumped into Andrew's path, his snarl moving to within inches of Andrew's face.

"Now you can go back to your nigger friends," he snapped.

Another boy moved next to his friend, each trying to get closer to their prey.

"Don't come back, coon," he ordered. "We were nice to you today."

Andrew looked straight ahead, his expression remaining stoic, trying to somehow hide the desperation and fear furiously smacking his mind. Escape? Survival? He kept walking.

****

Like parasites to a kill, several reporters and photographers stepped in front of Andrew, penetrating his existence with flashbulbs and words he tried not to comprehend.

"Excuse me," said one of the reporters. "We spoke this morning. *Virginian-Pilot*. Can I ask a few questions?"

A second reporter, from the Richmond newspaper, suddenly moved his shoulder in front of the Norfolk writer and callously pushed him away to the sway of the crowd.

"Did anyone hurt you today?" said the Richmond man.

Regaining his balance, the Norfolk reporter busted back into the moving interview.

"How was your first day?" he shouted, trying to best the pandemonium of the crowd while gaining ground with a vengeful shove against the rude reporter from Richmond. "Will you be back tomorrow?"

Andrew did not answer or make eye contact, but the *Virginian-Pilot* reporter was persistent in holding his position in front of the Richmond writer.

"Are you Heidelberg or Gonsouland?" asked the man from Norfolk.

Andrew still did not speak, now trying to evade the annoying flashes from about six or seven photographers. But, with each step, the crowd seemed to swell.

"Andrew, Andrew, over here," he distinctly heard from a distance. "Andrew, look this way."

Through the mayhem, Andrew thought he knew that voice and tried to change his course, the suffocation of the crowd playfully trying to alter his every move. Suddenly, Andrew saw the arms of a black adult waving for him.

"Andrew, over here," the man from the NAACP beckoned from a black limousine.

As if returning a kickoff, Andrew moved quickly toward the car, now seeing that its door was open and Mrs. Mason—beautiful Mrs. Mason—was sitting in the front passenger seat.

"Get in, Andrew," she said as he burst into the back seat, the man closing the door behind him.

"We're here to give you a ride home," she said. "Have you seen any of the other children?"

"No ma'am, not a soul all day," he said, his fractured adrenaline welcoming the blissful relief.

Outside the car, the crowd—laced with hate and gleeful amusement—continued the barrage of insults. Paying no attention to the chaos, Mrs. Mason smiled as she looked closely at Andrew.

"Are you all right, son?" she said with compassion and purpose. "How was your day?"

"I'm still alive," he said, his dry wit somehow returning.

Without warning, the back door flew open. Andrew was startled until he heard the NAACP man calling for more kids.

"Freddy, Olivia, over here," he instructed. "Mrs. Mason wants you in the car."

With Freddy and Olivia safe, the man closed the door and got behind the wheel.

"Let's go," said Mrs. Mason, "but drive slowly. We've still got four of my children out there. Look, up ahead, you see them. There's Delores and Pat, trying to get away from this crowd."

****

With the seven kids finally found and saved, the large black limo slowly left the disarray of hatred and started its journey toward their side of town. It was quiet inside, the students looking straight ahead, each lost in a somber and shell-shocked haze.

From the front seat, Mrs. Mason ultimately broke the silence.

"We'll take each of you to your homes," she said in her comforting voice. "We'll do this for a few days until things settle down. Make sure you look for us."

Mrs. Mason turned back around and said nothing more. The seven kids in the back remained quiet as the limo drove into the sanctity of the Black neighborhood.

Heidelberg

****

It was dark as the door opened in Andrew's room, the light from the kitchen and living room shining behind his mother. Still in his school clothes, Andrew was lying on his stomach, fast asleep on top of the covers of his bed. Mrs. Heidelberg gently shook his leg.

"Wake up, Son, it's supper time. I fried some chicken and baked some rolls especially for you."

Andrew raised his head and glanced at his mother, then rolled over on his back, still in a daze.

"Hey, Momma," he said quietly. "What time is it?"

"Dinner time. I know you're starving."

As Andrew got off his bed, his mother headed back for the kitchen, still talking in a soothing voice.

"Them white people wore your butt out today, didn't they, boy."

"You just don't know," Andrew muttered to himself, his face laced with anger.

As Andrew entered the kitchen, his brother and father looked up to size his mood. His mother turned from the stove with a hot chicken drumstick on the fork and looked closely at Andrew. Andrew looked back at his family, raised both arms in the air, and recited the baritone line from *Charlie Brown*.

"Why's everybody always pickin' on me?" he grumbled in a deep, worn voice.

"Cause you Charlie Brown and you're a clown," Kenny responded.

Andrew sat down at the table to his family's sweet sound of laughter.

"I heard a whole new version of dat song today," he said.

Gaines

****

Andrew was exhausted, deeply asleep the moment he hit his mattress ...

In the dream, Andrew was walking down a dirt path bordered by thick trees. It was foggy and strangely quiet. Suddenly, Andrew noticed several white faces staring at him from behind the branches and leaves of the trees.

Feeling his breath fall to his stomach, Andrew started to run, now rushing at full speed toward what looked like a large building. He stopped and pushed open the heavy door.

Inside the room, he tried focus through the darkness, but there were no windows ... only the noise of a deep and hollow growl. Slowly retreating, Andrew began to open the door, a faint streak of light revealing the presence of a large wolf, teeth snarling, eyes blood-red ... moving closer.

Andrew quickly backed out the door, slamming it behind him, making sure it was locked. Safe from the wolf, he knew he could outrun the white people, except now there were hundreds of them. As they silently moved closer, he noticed the knives, hammers, and bats ... and one shotgun, its cold touch now resting on Andrew's forehead.

He awakened in a cold sweat.

Chapter 11

It's Just a Matter of Time

E arly the next morning, both Andrew and his brother were asleep when their father excitedly entered their room holding a newspaper.

"Andrewkie, look at this! My son is famous."

Andrew pulled the covers over his head, but his father persistently pulled them back, holding the newspaper in front of his son's face.

"Pictures and stories on the front page of the newspaper," he said, his voice in a near frenzy. "And inside too. There's you and Freddy, right there in the *Virginian-Pilot*, the white people's paper. Boy, you look real good."

Andrew frowned and tried to cover his face with his hands to cut down the glare from the ceiling light.

"I don't wanna see no pictures, Daddy," he mumbled as his mother entered the room.

"Kenny, did you show your son his picture in the paper?"

"I was just telling him about how famous the Heidelberg name has become since yesterday," his father bragged.

Andrew's mom put her hand on the top of his covers and immediately yanked them back.

"Andrew, you and your brother didn't hear the phone? It woke me and your daddy up. It's been ringin' off the hook this morning."

"Even the Kingfish called," giggled Andrew's father as he once again began his famous impression of George "Kingfish" Stevens from the *Amos and Andy Show*.

"Holy makal der, Andy ..."

Andrew finally cracked a smile as he sat up in bed and began looking at the pictures in the paper.

"Daddy, dis really ain't funny," Andrew grumbled.

"You jus fill yoe mouth wit marbles," Mr. Heidelberg continued, incapable of not sounding like Kingfish. "Each day yoe take out a marble, and before you knows it, you'se lost all yoe marbles."

Mr. Heidelberg laughed while the rest of the family snickered.

"C'mon, boys, and get some breakfast in your belly," said Mrs. Heidelberg. "Your father can brag about his son all the way to work. And both you boys got classes."

As their parents left the room, Kenny got out of his bed and grabbed the newspaper from his younger brother's hands.

"Let me see what the white people are saying about y'all colored folks this morning," he said as he scanned the newspaper.

"Hey, Andrew, I think you lied to us, man," said Kenny as he began to read the article out loud.

"It says here dat, 'the 17 Negro children who broke da color line reported some friendliness and a few gaffs.'"

Kenny paused. "What da heck is a gaff?"

Andrew was trying not to listen.

"Goes on to say," said Kenny, "and I quote, 'everything went without incident, there was no disorder of any kind, it was a holiday atmosphere that comes with any first day of school.' And, oh, I like this part. It says that 'the colored children were treated just like anybody else.'"

Kenny stopped a moment, then raised his voice in excitement.

"Whoa, here's yo name right here. They quoted you, little brother."

Andrew raised his head, looking a bit puzzled.

"I didn't talk to nobody," he blurted.

"Says here you did," said Kenny. "Listen to this. 'Andrew Irwin Heidelberg said they called us some names, but it was quiet in class. I think I'll like it after things settle down.' Yep, dat's directly from yo mouth."

"Lemme see dat," said Andrew as he grabbed the newspaper from his brother.

Kenny pointed to the exact paragraph in the paper.

"See that? Andrew Irwin Heidelberg."

Andrew read the quote with a look of shocked amazement.

"I thought dem white boys was mean?" said Kenny. "But da paper says here y'all just one big happy family. Maybe I ought to go down dere wit you to Norview and have me some fun."

"Yeah, man, good idea," snarled Andrew. "In fact, you can take my place."

****

The second day, Freddy and Andrew took different directions after walking through the front entrance of Norview. Just inside the large entryway, the athletes standing at the wall stared at both boys, a few making various animal sounds. Their harmony sucked.

As Andrew attempted to maneuver the crowded hall, three white boys moved directly into his path. By their wild giddiness, Andrew immediately pegged them as freshmen.

"Look at this, Billy," said the first boy, "the nigger's back. Hey, did ya hear dat song yesterday?"

"Fe, fe, fi, fi, fo, fo, fum," sang Billy, "I smell a nigger in the auditorium ..."

"Yeah, Charlie Brown," said the third boy, "I thought you'd be back in Africa by now."

All three laughed as Andrew continued to walk, head down. The three freshmen stayed in front of him, walking backward.

"Yeah, boy, we kill niggers in this town," said the first kid, a cunning smile morphing into abhorrence.

Billy, meanwhile, acted as if he were about to shoot an imaginary rifle, aiming directly at Andrew.

"Got me a Coon in my sites," he giggled.

Andrew tried to get past the freshmen, but they continually blocked his way. Finally, with his classroom in view, he faked the three boys to the right and maneuvered to the left and through the door to his homeroom, leaving them to stumble and curse.

He moved quickly to his seat next to the window, the desks on each side of him empty. The teacher had not yet arrived, although about half the class was scattered around the room. Andrew opened a book and pretended to read.

"Hey Andy," said one of the boys.

Andrew knew the voice. It was one of the kids who had given him trouble the first day.

"Andy, seriously, let's talk."

Andrew hesitated but turned around to partially see the kid leaning toward him.

"Tell me," he said. "Is it true that niggers, I mean, colored people ..."

The others in the class burst out laughing as if this was great entertainment.

"Is it true," the kid continued, "that colored people have tails tucked in their clothes?"

Andrew turned away, directing his focus back to his book as the laughter heightened.

****

After lunch, the hallways were relatively quiet as most students were outside. As Andrew approached the gymnasium for his PE class, he saw a white student standing under one of the large team football pictures, also waiting for the gym door to open. He looked up at Andrew and smiled.

"Hey, how's it going?" he said.

Andrew was hesitant, figuring this to be the start of yet another crude ambush.

"Um fine," he said, keeping eye contact at a glance. "What about you?"

There was a touch of silence as both looked again at the gym door.

"I'm good," said the white boy, putting out his hand to shake. "My name is Bob."

Andrew cautiously shook hands.

"Andrew," he said.

"I wish they'd open the gym during lunch," said Bob. "I'd love to shoot some baskets."

"Yeah, that would be nice," said Andrew, still guarded.

"I saw you here yesterday, some guys giving you a hard time," said Bob. "I guess you're getting a lot of that."

"Yeah, way too much," said Andrew, his voice beginning to ease as his eyes made contact with the white kid.

"Sort of surprises me," said Bob. "We just moved here a couple of weeks ago from San Diego. My dad's in the Navy. In California, all the schools are integrated. Norfolk's a great place, but some things are kinda weird around here."

"I ain't never been to California," said Andrew. "I been living here all my life."

"I'm not saying things are perfect out there, just a lot different."

"Do you play basketball?" asked Andrew as if this might be an actual friendship.

"Yeah, I'm okay," said Bob. "I just wish I was about eight inches taller and had a better hook shot ... you know, the kind that never misses."

Both boys laughed.

"I play a lotta basketball too," said Andrew, "but football's my real game."

"Yeah, I like football," said Bob. "Before we moved, me and my Dad went to Los Angeles and saw the Rams play the Chicago Bears. Jon Arnett, Joe Marconi, Lamar Lundy ... Rams won 41-35."

"Man, I like da Baltimore Colts and da Chicago Cardinals best," said Andrew.

"The Cardinals? You know they finished last?"

"Yeah, but they got Ollie Matson," said Andrew. "He's great."

"Yeah, he's good all right," said Bob. "So, let me see, you like the Colts cause they're the champs."

"Naw, man," shot back Andrew in a pronounced and kidding way. "I like Lenny Moore."

"Oh yeah, he's fast," said Bob, "and puts all that tape up his shoes."

"Yeah, man," said Andrew, "makes him look like he got on spats. Dat's cool."

As the boys chatted, several white male students approached the closed gym, stopping to glare, but saying nothing.

"So, who's your favorite player?" Andrew asked Bob.

"That's easy," he said. "I'll give you a hint. He's the best player in college."

"No idea," said Andrew.

"Number 20 on LSU, Billy Cannon."

"Yeah, he's good," said Andrew, "but nobody can stop Jim Brown."

"I wouldn't wanna get in front of him," said Bob as the bell rang and the gym door opened. They entered, still talking.

****

Andrew's friendship with Bob was the only respite during the first few weeks of school, his world punctuated by the constant barrage of hatred. Spit wads and insults flew through the classrooms, teachers ignoring the obvious. But class was easy compared to the hallways where the stares and taunts never ceased.

"Hey Tommy, do you think it's gonna rain today?" said a white kid Andrew was attempting to skirt past.

"Hmm," said Tommy, "I do think it's gonna rain. I see a black cloud right now."

Andrew looked directly at the two weathermen, squinting his eyes to denote that their joke was particularly lame.

"Crazy nigger," one giggled as the other continued to roar.

Andrew clenched his jaw and kept moving. He realized that, over time, his attitude was changing, having moved from the early days of embarrassment and humiliation to an enhanced feeling of total disdain toward whites, an enemy deserving no trust or respect.

****

Andrew entered the boys' bathroom, moving directly to one of the urinals. The bathroom was empty except for two older kids smoking in front of the last stall. One was wearing a white t-shirt with a pack of Lucky Strike cigarettes rolled up in his right sleeve. The other wore a black leather jacket and was twirling a long chain. Andrew then noticed a third kid, also dressed like a thug, standing near the back sink. Each of them looked too old to be in high school.

"What are you doing in here, nigger?" snarled the kid in the t-shirt.

"Yeah, nigger, we could kill your black ass," said the guy with the chain.

"Yeah, why don't we do just that," added the third thug.

Stationed at the urinal, Andrew had no choice but to finish. Despite the impending danger, he tried to appear calm. He finished, zipped his pants, and turned around. The three bigots had blocked the exit, one still twirling his chain. After moving to the sink to slowly wash his hands, Andrew had no other choice but to walk directly toward them. The boy with the chain stepped in front of the other two.

At that moment, from behind the three hoodlums, a tough-looking man in a brown suit abruptly entered the bathroom. Immediately gauging the situation, he moved to the center of the conflict where he stood nose-to-nose with the chain swinger.

"Put out your cigarettes and leave, right now," demanded Andrew T. Leidy, the assistant principal who was obviously well-trained to squash punks and hoods. "I told you three before to stay off school grounds. I catch you here again, I will call the police."

With a new swagger to his step, Andrew walked right between Mr. Leidy and the tough guys.

"Thank you, Mr. Leidy?" he said, never in his life so happy to see a white man.

Heidelberg

****

Mostly, Andrew was alone, his anger seething, building with every encounter. Don't think about it, he tried to tell himself, constantly repeating the advice from the NAACP—keep your head high, but don't show any expression, don't make eye contact, don't look at white girls, don't talk, don't fight, don't get expelled, don't react to taunts, be invisible, don't be who you really are ...

And what about God? A caring God would have never let this happen. A true and powerful God would have sent the white bigots straight to Hell, every one of them. Call a kid a nigger and, zap, you're fried.

At times, Andrew was as angry at God as he was at the whites.

He also, for the first time in his life, was becoming consumed by a feeling of inferiority. He was ashamed of himself, wondering why he had been so unlucky to be born black. He looked in the mirror, stared at his hands ... it was truly a curse.

There was no way he would share his self-doubt with the NAACP, which was now holding meetings twice a week to nurture the Norfolk 17. Of course, the NAACP knew the fragility of the situation. Their idea was to keep the kids focused, provide support, remind them of their cause ... and try to repair the esteem that each day was being hammered beyond recognition.

But if he were white ... if Andrew Heidelberg was white, he would at least have friends at Norview.

Out of the far corner of his eyes, Andrew watched the students interact within their exclusive circle of whiteness. And when it was just them intermingling, they all seemed to be having such a great time.

What would it be like to be white? He wondered, and then became overpowered by guilt.

108

****

Walking to Norview on a cold morning in early March, Andrew was taking a shortcut through Mamie Homes, a Black housing development between Chesapeake Manor and Chesapeake Gardens. Exiting from the path that shot through a wooded area, he saw one of the city's red and yellow transit buses carrying students to Booker T. Washington High School. One of the kids, a friend who played football with Andrew and lived several blocks away, opened his bus window.

"Hey, white boy," he yelled with a huge grin on his face, "Don't be late for school."

Several other kids, who also knew Andrew, pulled down their windows, laughing and having great fun at his expense.

"Hey, Bird, don't let dem white boys give ya any trouble," one bellowed.

"You better hurry up, Bird," yelled a third friend. "If you late, dey gon whip ya butt wit 50 lashes."

Andrew gave the group a halfhearted smile and wave.

"Don't get hung, Bird," one of the kids yelled before the bus turned the corner and disappeared.

****

As he approached the gymnasium, Andrew saw Bob standing near the door, his face turned to the wall.

"Hey, what's up man?" said Andrew, approaching from behind.

Bob slowly, with humbled embarrassment, turned toward Andrew.

"Oh, man, what happened?" asked Andrew, his smile replaced by horror.

Bob was battered, his face horribly disfigured with black-and-blue swollen eyes, one totally shut. He looked as if he had repeatedly been hit with a baseball bat.

"They beat me up, Andrew, because I've been talking to you," Bob mumbled, barely able to speak. "I can't even tell you what they said, except that the next time is gonna be worse ... if they see us talking again."

"That's all right, man," said Andrew, his eyes beginning to tear. "Don't even worry bout it. I understand."

Bob looked down, beaten and somber.

"I'm sorry," he said, putting his hand over the closed eye and walking away.

Andrew angrily looked around the hall, but there was no one in sight.

****

Mrs. Tucker had instructed the kids in her class to turn to page 56 in their science book.

"Today, we are going to learn how people see colors," she said. "Can someone tell me what they see?"

One of the white girls was the first to raise her hand, claiming she saw the word "COLOR" embedded within a bunch of circles in all different colors. Mrs. Tucker asked if everyone saw the same picture, and they all agreed, except Andrew. He bent his head forward to get a closer look at the page, but he just could not see what everyone was talking about. He hesitated, reluctantly raising his hand.

"Yes, Andy, do you have a question?" said Mrs. Tucker.

Everyone in the class, as expected, immediately turned their focus on Andrew, sitting alone by the window.

"I don't see the word COLOR," he said.

"Well, Andrew, what word do you see?"

"I see ONION."

"Onion?" The class howled with laughter.

"Did you bring one of your books from Booker T, Andy?" some kid asked above the roar.

"They ain't got books at Booker T," said another.

Mrs. Tucker raised her hand for silence, giving a stern look to the most vocal boys.

"Come to order, class," she said. "Everyone turn to the next page and read the note in bold print at the bottom. See what it says. "If color perception is normal, you will see the word COLOR. However, if you are color-blind, you will see the word ONION.'"

It took a moment for the concept to register, but laughter broke forth again.

"Oh no, Andy is COLORED blind," yelled one kid.

"Andy, did you know you were COLORED blind?" added another as Mrs. Tucker attempted to regain control of the room.

****

Standing in front of Bobby's house in Oakwood, Andrew repeated the sad story.

"All I saw was the word ONION," he moaned before imitating the reaction of the class. "Oh, Andy, you COLORED blind."
Bobby could only laugh.

"That is sorta funny, Bird," he said.

"Not to me, man. Dem whiteys don't ever let up. Dey always laughin or callin me names. Err'body think da nigga funny. It ain't even funny. I hate em, Knuck, I hate em."

Bobby's laughter died as Andrew's anger swelled.

"Like da utter day," Andrew continued, "they really got to

111

me. Dey come out wit crap like 'why do colored people talk so slow and lazy?' Like I sound like dat damn Steppin Fetchit. Dey thought it was the funniest thing in da world. I ain't never been laughed at so much. I bet dey musta laughed 15 minutes. You think I talk lazy, Knuck?"

"Man, I say dis again," said Bobby. "You sound more like dem whiteys every day."

"Naw, man, um talkin bout talkin lazy, like real lazy talk, Knuck. For instance, you go to Boogga T."

Andrew added emphasis by pronouncing the words slowly and correctly.

"You go to BOOKER T."

"Das right," said Bobby, "and I am damn sho glad I do."

"Naw, you missin it, Knuck. Say like the white boy in my English class. I'on know his name. I cain't even tell em apart most of da time. But he said to me, 'Andy, where is Booker T?' I told em it's downtown on Prince Anne Road."

"Yeah, so, dat's right," said Bobby. "Boogga T is downtown on Prince Anne Road."

"Naw, Bobby, that's what I mean by lazy talk. Cause ain't no such thing as Prince Anne. Anne ain't no prince. It's PRINCESS Anne Road."

Bobby didn't even bother to process this lesson in proper articulation.

"Dey just talkin shit, Bird. Sides, white folks always sayin Y'ALL. Y'all do this, y'all do that, y'all come over, y'all go ta hell. Dat's lazy talk."

"You right, Knuck, I think we talk just fine."

Bobby shook his head in agreement.

"I'on know how *y'all* take all dat crap all da time," he said. "You and Freddy, Olivia and dem. Man, y'all oughtta git together and kick some butt."

"Git together? Man, once I git in dem halls, I'on even see none of dem. All I see is white people. Dey must have a plan to keep us apart. I'on know why, but dey do."

"Well, you only been der three months," said Bobby, "and you still got two months left til summer."

"An den I got three more years after dat," said Andrew. "I'on know if um gon make it, Knuck."

"Naw, you'll make it, Bird. If anybody can find daylight, it's you."

****

Andrew was certain that he had figured it out. The school officials purposely kept the colored kids separated. It had to be a carefully planned scheme—divide and conquer, get them alone and they'll break. Like everything else the white man did, Andrew deduced, it was born in evil.

One day in late spring, turning onto Sewells Point Road after school, Andrew spotted Patricia Godbolt walking ahead of him. Pat was 17, the oldest of the black students attending Norview. Andrew ran to catch up with her.

"Hey, Pat, how's it going?"

She looked hurried, continuing to walk at a brisk pace.

"Fine Andrew. How are you doing?"

"Okay I guess," he said, moving quickly to keep up. "I was just tellin one of my boys dat I'on never see any of the other black kids in school."

"Yeah, I don't either," she said.

"That must be some kind of plan," he said.

Pat shook her head in agreement but didn't say anything. They continued walking along the fence in silence, passing Perkins Market and crossing Widgeon Road into the Colored section. Pat broke the silence.

"Andrew, I got to go to the bathroom."

Somewhat confounded by the statement, he did not respond.

"I've been holding it all day," she repeated with hurried emphasis as they reached a large, vacant field along the road. "I can't wait any longer. I really gotta go."

She burst into a full run toward the two-foot-tall grass, stopping about 30 yards from Andrew, dropping her books, raising her skirt, pulling down her underpants, and squatting slightly to relieve herself. Andrew stood at the edge of the path, his eyes turned away, his mouth wide open. Finally finished, Pat pulled up her underpants, straightened her skirt, picked up her books, and returned.

They continued walking toward their homes, neither saying a word.

Chapter 12

Do You Wanna Dance?

S harply dressed, Andrew entered the front doors of Norview High School for another day of torment. As always, the inside wall was lined with athletes looking cool at their early-morning hangout, most wearing white cardigan sweaters with the big blue "N" on the lower left pocket. One of the jocks, Bake Banks, was waiting for Andrew.

"Hey, Andy," he said in a quite friendly voice.

"Yeah?" said Andrew, his mental guard already on full alert.

As Bake moved toward Andrew, he smiled and casually raised his right hand to the left side of Andrew's head. Andrew immediately pulled back, raising his own arm to thwart Bake's touch.

"Get your hand off," Andrew began to say as he suddenly felt a liquid running down the side of his head. He instinctively wiped his head, bringing the liquid to his nose ... the smell was disgustingly horrible, an odor like raw sewage that seemed to immediately spread throughout the hall, students wincing at the stench.

"Oh God," said one of the jocks, "what the hell is that awful smell?"

The athletes pulled back, nearly all holding their noses as Bake smiled in arrogant delight.

Andrew dropped his books and peered into his adversary's eyes.

"Um gon break your jaw," said Andrew, putting both hands up to fight, only to trigger about 25 athletes to move quickly toward him. But, as they surrounded Andrew, Mr. Charles Perdue jumped into the middle of the crowd, grabbing Andrew by the arm.

"Okay, boys, break it up," said the principal. "Everybody, get to your classes. Andy, you come with me." Mr. Perdue gasped. "What the heck is that smell?"

****

Entering the main office, Mr. Perdue told Andrew to sit on the long bench across from the counter.

"My God, Mr. Perdue, that smell," complained one of the secretaries as the other two assistants covered their noses, squinting in disbelief.

"Andy, sit right here until I come back," ordered Mr. Perdue as he headed for his private office, slamming the door behind him. The women were madly trying to open every window as a male teacher entered the office.

"Good morning Miss ... oh ..."

The teacher held his nose, looked at Andrew with total disgust, and quickly exited. A moment later, a female teacher tried to enter.

"Lord," she screamed, immediately turning around.

At the door, she ran into another teacher, pushing him back.

"Don't even go in there," she said, throwing the door shut.

Andrew was once again humiliated.

****

Andrew sat in front of the principal's desk as Mr. Perdue opened the window, holding a handkerchief at his nose.

"Andrew, I am told you threatened another student out there in the hall. You know that any such conduct at Norview will not be tolerated."

"But, Mr. Perdue, he came after me."

"Did you provoke him?"

"No sir, all I did was walk in the door."

Mr. Perdue gave Andrew a stern stare.

"Well, I will investigate this matter thoroughly," he said. "I will let you know if your actions deserve a suspension. Do you understand?"

"Yes sir," said Andrew. "May I go home now, so I can wash this stuff off and change my clothes?"

Mr. Perdue answered without hesitation.

"No, you can't go home," he grumbled. "As soon as the bell rings, you go down to the boys' bathroom and wash that odor off your head."

Alone in the school bathroom, embarrassment mixed with fury, Andrew tried desperately to clean the side of his face and hair with soap and water. He scrubbed over and over, but the scent would not wash away.

****

The next afternoon, Mrs. Heidelberg was standing with Andrew in their living room, holding a piece of paper from school.

"I can't believe it, I really can't believe this," she said in anger. "Some stupid white boy pours some, some, I don't even know what to call it. Stink, or worse than that. I can't even get it outta

117

your clothes. They make you stay there the whole day; don't even let you go home and change. I don't believe this."

She lifted the sheet of paper to her eye level, shaking it in anger.

"To top it off, they say you're suspended for two days and the white boy that started it, all he gets is a *stern warning*? I don't believe it. I don't believe it. Did Mr. Perdue know that I had to burn all your clothes?"

"No ma'am," said Andrew.

"The note says that you threatened the boy. Is that true? What did you say?"

"All I said was dat I was gon break his jaw, and dat was only after he poured dat stuff on me."

Mrs. Heidelberg did not process her son's reason.

"So, you had to be big bad Andrew, huh? What the devil were you thinking, anyway? Never mind, you weren't thinking."

Mrs. Heidelberg stopped, suddenly realizing she was being harsh out of frustration. She took a deep breath and moved closer to Andrew, opening her arms to embrace him.

"I know it's hard, Son, I know," she said in a soft and loving voice. "I just get so mad with those people I just want to scream. I'm always proud of you, you know that. I love you, Son."

They hugged for the longest time, his mother softly patting his back.

****

During lunch period, Andrew had wandered outside to check out Norview's immaculate athletic facilities. On the baseball diamond—with its high mound, manicured infield, and lush green-grass outfield—he noticed three students taking batting practice. Matt Crawford, an athlete who had taunted Andrew on several occasions, was pitching to a catcher and hitter.

Quietly approaching from behind the third-base dugout, Andrew leaned on the four-foot fence with his arms crossed. Crawford's brisk fastball and nasty curve had the hitter off-balance and guessing. Crawford's heat and control were impressive.

Realizing Andrew was watching, Crawford suddenly stopped his wind-up, snapped the ball into his mitt, and walked off the mound toward the intruder.

"What are you looking at, nigger?" he growled.

With Andrew pretending not to hear, Crawford took a few steps closer, heatedly pointing his glove.

"I said, what the hell are you doing here, nigger?"

"I'm out for a walk," snapped Andrew.

"Well, why doncha get the fuck outta here before I bust your damn head with this ball," Crawford fired back.

Andrew defiantly stood his ground.

"If you think you're man enough to ..."

Andrew did not complete the sentence as he realized the ball was coming straight for his eyes at about 90 miles an hour. He ducked, barely escaping serious injury. Getting back up, Andrew saw the two other white boys running to restrain Crawford, who struggled to break free from their grasp.

"Take it easy, Matt," said the catcher. "You'll get thrown out of school."

"Are you crazy?" said Andrew, his voice powerful and angry. "You could've killed me."

"I'm gonna tear you apart," screamed Crawford, still attempting to pull away from his friends' grasp. "What're you gonna do about it?"

"Um gon kick your ass," yelled Andrew, shaking the fence. "Whatchu think um gon do?"

"You just meet me after school, nigger, today. I'll show you whose ass is gonna get kicked."

Having pulled free from his friends, Crawford pointed across the street to Perkins Grocery Store.

"Perkins, 3:30, your ass is dead, nigger."

"I'll be there, sucker."

Andrew turned and headed toward the school building.

As he approached the area where Crawford's baseball had landed, he heard the catcher yelling to him.

"Hey, nigger, throw the ball back," the kid commanded.

Andrew walked right past the baseball, not even bothering to look down.

****

Andrew was sitting at his desk during his last class of the day. About 10 minutes before the final bell, a girl entered the room with a note for the teacher.

"Andy Heidelberg, the principal wants to see you in his office," said the teacher. "He wants you to bring your books."

The other students made their usual faces and whispers as Andrew gathered his books and left.

****

Mr. Perdue greeted Andrew with a smile.

"Andy, I think you better stay here in my office for a few minutes after the last bell."

"Did I do something wrong, sir?"

"No, you didn't do anything wrong. But I heard that there might be some trouble brewing. You aware of any trouble?"

"No sir," said Andrew.

The principal studied Andrew's face.

"I see," he said. "Well, you'll be here for a little while, so you can do your homework. I also have some letters with your name on them. They're from all over the United States, and even places like Yugoslavia, Canada, and England. We opened them already because they're addressed to Norview. It's okay for you to read them, but we'll keep them here."

Andrew looked at the letters and started to pull one from its open envelope.

"You got some fans out there, Andy," said Mr. Perdue, uncommonly jovial.

****

Early that evening, as Andrew was walking toward the basketball court near his home, he heard Freddy from a distance.

"Hey, Heidelberg, wait up."

Andrew stopped.

"You okay?" said Freddy, putting out his hands for Andrew to pass the basketball.

"Um jus doin the best I can wit what I got," was a phrase Andrew had proudly borrowed from his father.

"No, really, what's up?" said Freddy.

"Well, really, it's the same soup, just warmed over," said Andrew, pushing a bounce pass right to Freddy's chest. "Welcome to 'Call Andy A Nigger Week' at Norview High School."

Freddy laughed, as he passed the ball back to Andrew.

"Oh yeah," said Freddy, "I meant to ask you what the hell was going on after school?"

Andrew looked puzzled.

"After school? Dog if I know, Freddy. You tell me."

"Boy," said Freddy, "there must have been a couple hundred

white kids out there by Perkins Market."

"Hmmm," said Andrew, still playing naïve.

"I heard them talking as I passed by," said Freddy. "They were saying something like, 'We gonna kill that nigger if he shows up.' They were foaming from the mouth like a pack of wild dogs. Where the heck were you?"

"I had to stay back and talk to Mr. Perdue," said Andrew. "So, who do you think they were waiting for?"

"I don't know," said Freddy, "but since you're not dead, apparently it wasn't you."

"Man, I can't wait for summer," said Andrew.

****

Finally! The bell had just sounded on the last day of school, the halls filled with excited students. Trying not to look at anyone, Andrew walked out the front door onto the steps, past a group of white boys who were laughing and smiling.

"See you later, nigger," one of them said. "Don't get sunburned this summer."

"Niggers and flies, I do despise," said another. "The more I see niggers, the more I like flies ..."

The white boys were lost in high hilarity. Andrew was long past them.

Chapter 13

Escape to Summer

Bobby and the Emeralds were magic, their soulful sound of rhythm and blues igniting the crowd at many of the talent shows hosted by Norfolk's colored recreation centers. The summer audiences usually consisted of about a hundred Black teenagers. At this show, Betty Jean was most impressed with the Emeralds' smooth dance steps and their flawless harmonies spanning from the *Book of Love* to *Tears on My Pillow*.

After the last act, Bobby and the Emeralds stood on stage with six other groups as the judges made their picks.

"Ladies and gentlemen," said the MC into the microphone. "I'm proud to announce the winner of the 1960 Titustown Talent Show, those outstanding young men from ... uh, what's that place? Oh yeah, from Oakwood, it's Bobby and the Emeralds."

As the crowd went wild, Betty Jean ran up the steps onto the stage to give Andrew a hug and kiss. She also hugged Bobby, who seemed to have his own fan club.

"Ya'll were great," she said.

"Yes, I was," said Andrew.

"You was?" interrupted Bobby. "Bird, you cain't even keep yo pitch."

"But I can harmonize oh so nice," said Andrew, puckering his lips for another big kiss from Betty Jean. She, however, pulled back with a smile and gave him a fake wop on the forehead.

"Bird," interrupted Bobby, "if you kiss like you sing, I pity da pooh girl."

"Knuck, I have many talents," bragged Andrew.

Bobby cleared his throat as if preparing to say something profound.

"I have many talents," said Bobby in a dead-on mimic of Andrew.

He then returned to his normal voice.

"Damn, Bird, I tol you befoe, you sound just like dem white boys when you sing. I cain't tell da difference tween you and dem Everly Brothers."

The laughter from Andrew and Betty further inspired Bobby.

"Hey, Bird Dog, you on the wrong trail," warbled Bobby with a rather dry and out-of-key version to the Everly Brothers number one hit from the year before.

"Johnny is a joker, he's a bird."

Andrew, of course, immediately harmonized, adding his smooth dancing impression of the Everly Brothers.

"A very funny joker," they both warbled, "he's a dog."

"Lord, us white boys sho got da moves," laughed Bobby.

Andrew put the skids to his dance steps, then sang in his slowest and deepest white voice.

"Out in the west Texas town of El Paso ..."

"Andrew Heidelberg," kidded Betty Jean, "You are really crazy."

"Naw," said Bobby, "he crazy for real."

"Oh, hey, Knuck, I forgot to tell ya I saw Joe Austin yesterday," said Andrew. "He say you and me so good, we gotta move up to da senior league."

"Dat's alright," said Bobby. "We still gon kick errebody butt up der."

"You got dat right," said Andrew, going into his football motion. "We be playin wit Freddy and all da big boys. Here come Lenny Moore, taped up shoes and all, fakin you outta yo jock wit my sweet moves."

You two ever think about anything other than football?" said Betty Jean, looking a bit whimsical.

"Yeah, I think baseball most of da time," said Bobby. "Dat's da game dat takes skill plus brains."

Bobby playfully slugged Andrew on the shoulder as they both turned their attention to Betty Jean, who suddenly seemed disinterested.

"I guess the one thing I don't like about football," she said with a pout. "It means I'll be back at Granby, all alone."

"Oh Lord, I was trying not to think bout dat," said Andrew. "I don't know how you make it over dere by yo self, baby."

"C'mon now," said Bobby, "ya'll out there fightin for truth, justice, and the American way. Cain't be dat bad. Dem white people gotta be used to y'all by now."

"You're right, Bobby," said Betty Jean. "That's why I've been nominated for Homecoming Queen."

"Yeah," added Andrew, "and I plan on goin da whole day without somebody callin me a nigger."

"Well, it ain't today, nigga," said Bobby, "cause ya cain't dance and ya sing like a white boy."

****

Andrew and Bobby were sitting on the bench at the corner next to the Heidelberg's front yard.

"Man, we saw Marvin last night," said Bobby. "Me and him,

Lil Joe and Calvin were messin round singin. You know sumpin, Bird, we sounded pretty good without you."

Bobby laughed, but Andrew only glared.

"I tried to call you," Bobby continued, "but yo line was busy all night. I know ya had ta be talkin to Betty Jean, huh?"

"Maybe," said Andrew.

"Oh, man, I knew it was sumpin I had to tell ya," blurted Bobby. "We might be doin a radio commercial next week. Marvin know dis DJ name David B. or sumpin like dat down at WNOR, and he wanna hear us sing the theme song for his show."

Bobby poked Andrew in the ribs.

"Course, we sounded so good last night without yo dried out voice, we might not need ya no more," Bobby continued. "Thousands of people gon be listening, so we sho don need you losin yo tune again."

"Yeah, Knuck, don't forget we ain't always been Bobby and the Emeralds," said Andrew. "Member, we were originally Heidel and the Idols."

"Yeah, Heidel and the Idols," chuckled Bobby. "Who in da hell came up wit dat stupid name?"

****

Andrew and Betty Jean were alone on the front porch of her home, the radio turned low in the background to the romantic sounds of *Maybe* by The Chantels.

"I'm glad Bobby and Barbara get along so well," said Betty Jean. "He can spend all the time over at her house he wants. It gives me a chance to spend more time alone with you."

Betty Jean leaned softly back onto Andrew's shoulder.

"With school startin up again next week," she said, "I'm gonna really miss seeing you."

Betty Jean put her arms around Andrew, squeezed him tightly, and took a deep breath.

"We still got the weekends," he said. "And who knows, maybe you can come see some of my football games."

Betty Jean lifted her head from Andrew's chest and looked at him with somewhat sad eyes.

"Sure, we got so much time," she pouted. "With all that homework, I'll be lucky to see you at all."

"Well, I sure ain't lookin forward to goin back to Norview, and you gon be all alone at Granby. Man, dat's gotta be de worse."

"Remember what the NAACP kept telling us over and over," said Betty Jean. "If we wanna pave the way for others, it means being unhappy at times."

"Yeah, I know all about that paving stuff," said Andrew. "I just always thought high school was spose ta be fun."

****

Singing, playing sports, kissing Betty Jean ... there were moments when it seemed that the long and hot summer might never end. But Andrew knew it would. The closer school approached, the more anxious his manner, a sickeningly hollow reminder that he was about to return to the deepest dungeon of Hell.

Chapter 14
Back to School Blues

Approaching the front door of Norview on the first day of his sophomore year, Andrew was suddenly surrounded by four white boys, two walking on each side.

"Hello, nigger, we didn't think you'd be coming back," said the first boy with a friendly smile.

"Nice suntan you got there, boy," said the second.

They both laughed, but a third boy was more serious.

"This gon be yo last year here, tar baby," he threatened. "Maybe yo last day."

"Cause we gon lynch all you niggers," growled the first boy, his grin holding strong.

"Startin wit you," said the other.

As Andrew and the four bigots reached the front steps of the school, two of the boys rushed to reach the doorway first.

"You must be lost, nigger," said the second boy, pointing his arm in the opposite direction. "Africa's back that way."

As Andrew reached the door, one of the boys jumped in front of him, went through the door, and purposely pulled it shut. Andrew tugged for a moment until the boy let go, then opened the door and entered the school.

"Great to be back," Andrew mumbled to himself.

****

That afternoon, Andrew reached the top of the second-floor stairs and turned the hallway corner. As he approached his classroom, three white boys stood outside the door of an adjacent class, one looking at Andrew with a huge smile. Andrew recognized him as one of the boys who had hassled him that morning.

"Good afternoon, nigger," said the boy with a courteous greeting as his friends broke into laughter.

Nothing had changed from his freshman year. Aisles would open in the hallway, girls would jump at the sight of him, seats remained empty around him, spit wads flew past, and he was continually called a cluster of crude names—coon, mau mau, spook, spear chucker, and, of course, the granddaddy of them all, nigger.

And every afternoon, as he approached his class on the second floor, the same three boys stood outside the door of an adjacent class, Mister Smiles repeating exactly what he had said the day before.

"Good afternoon, nigger."

The other two boys would laugh, and Andrew would walk past the trio as if they were not there. Three more years, he thought, and then he could escape this nonsense and join the Marines.

For now, the best part of Andrew's routine was playing football for the Colts. Andrew starred with Freddy and Bobby on what was easily the best team in the Colored Recreation Bureau's senior league.

But while football was a momentary break, school never seemed to end.

"Good afternoon, nigger," said the smiling bigot as Andrew headed for his second-floor class, the other two boys laughing in unison.

****

Walking home after school, Andrew stopped by the fence along Sewells Point Road to watch Norview's junior varsity playing an afternoon football game against Granby. The unbeaten JV Pilots were impressive, and they wore the same great uniforms as the varsity, except nobody had to share jerseys.

Andrew knew most of the JV players were his age. He studied their speed, moves, talent. Without doubt, he was better than anyone on the field.

****

Reaching the top of the second-floor stairs and turning the hallway corner on his way to his classroom, Andrew saw the same three white boys standing at the same spot. As always, a big smile came across the talkative kid's face, but before he could speak, Andrew happily greeted him.

"Good afternoon, nigger," said Andrew.

Immediately, the other two white boys turned to their boisterous friend, pointing their fingers at him, and laughing hilariously.

"Did you hear that?" said one of the kids to their stunned friend. "Andy called you a nigger."

The entire floor was now laughing.

"He called you a nigger," rattled the third kid.

130

Andrew momentarily joined the laughter, then walked into his classroom.

****

Andrew was entering the main door of Norview as the first bell was about to ring. After passing the athletes, lined up in their usual spot, he approached a group of freshman boys talking near the center of the hallway.

"Hey guys," said one of the freshmen, "looks like we might get some rain today."

"Why do you say that?" said a second kid.

"Cause I see a black cloud passing by," said the first boy as the group chuckled.

Andrew walked directly to them and stopped.

"Naw, it ain't gon rain," he said. "There's way too many white clouds hangin around."

Andrew smiled and walked to class amidst great laughter. He had somehow stumbled onto a brilliant niche—turning humor into a weapon. Okay, it bordered on self-deprecation, but it was working ...

****

Andrew reached the top of the second-floor stairs and turned the hallway corner. Something was strangely out of place, he thought, suddenly realizing that the three white adversaries were nowhere to be seen. He slowed down, looked for them, and smiled.

If life at Norview High School was starting to change, it was barely noticeable. Okay, the taunts and mocking had simmered a bit as his sophomore year progressed, but they still existed.

131

"Nigger" did not disappear, nor did spit wads cease flying. He still sat alone. He still kept his defenses on high alert.

If humor had won any battles, it only agitated the war in his mind. Andrew did not trust whites, nor did he like them.

Finally, school broke for summer. He was once again free.

****

Going to Titustown to visit Betty Jean and her friend, Barbara, on a muggy summer afternoon, Andrew and Bobby walked down the middle of Little Creek Road. The subject had jumped from a lengthy discussion concerning who was the better baseball player—Willie Mays or Hank Aaron—to Andrew's brother, Kenny, dropping out of Norfolk State and joining the Army.

As they always did when cars approached, they would move to the side of the road and put up their thumb for a possible ride.

"Hey, Bird, I heard all dem guys uptown want Freddy ta come play football wit dem at Booga T dis year," said Bobby.

"Well, um sho dey do, Knuck," said Andrew. "Freddy can run dat ball. But how's he gon play wit Booga T and he goes to Norview?"

"He gon transfer, turkey," said Bobby.

Andrew took a moment to process the news.

"Naw," he finally said. "Heck, me and Freddy should be goin out for Norview."

On instinct, Andrew tucked his arm as if he had a football in hand, doing a few of his best moves in the street. Seeing a car on its way, Bobby grabbed Andrew.

"Go head and dance yo butt out there in fronta dose cars. You ain't gon play wit Norview or nobody else."

Standing at the side of the road as the car zoomed by, Andrew continued making his point.

"Norview would never lose if me and Freddy played for dem."

"Dey neva lose anyway, Bird," said Bobby. "But dat don't matter cause dey ain't gon let y'all play. Freddy knows if he wanna play ball, he betta go ta Booga T."

"Well, um sho gon ask him what's up," said Andrew as both boys put up their thumbs for another passing car that did not even slow down.

Back home in Chesapeake Manor that evening, Andrew stood outside of Freddy's house and called for him. After a few minutes, Freddy came outside.

"Bird, when are you gonna learn to knock on the door?" said Freddy, grabbing Andrew as if he was going to tackle and pick him up.

Andrew pulled from Freddy's grasp.

"I heard you were transferrin to Booga T, man."

Caught off guard, Freddy looked back to see if anyone was within hearing distance.

"Who told you that? I didn't say anything to anybody."

"Well, Knuck told me everybody on Booga T wants you on dat team," said Andrew. "Man, I thought you and me was gonna go out for Norview."

Freddy stared at Andrew in disbelief.

"What? You gotta be kidding me. I'm not trying out for nothing at Norview. Are you forgetting that we can't even go in the stadium? You think they're gonna let us play football?"

"I'on know, man," said Andrew. "I thought we'd go out."

"Well, you go ahead my friend," said Freddy. "Check it out for yourself and good luck, I wish you well. I'm going to Booker T where I know I can play."

Andrew looked away. "What about the NAACP, and all we've been through?"

"Man, this is my last year of high school," said Freddy. "I know some people are gonna say that I quit Norview, and I know what we're trying to do and all that, but I gotta play football, Bird. You know that."

Andrew looked back at his friend.

"Yeah, man, I know."

Chapter 15

The Tryout

On August 22, 1960, Andrew entered a gymnasium filled with prospective football players. As he approached several Norview coaches seated at a desk set up in the middle of the gym floor, seemingly all the white boys stared at him, but nobody made any comments.

"Hey, Coach," said Andrew. "Is this where I sign up for football?"

"Yes sir," the equipment coach said in an upbeat voice. "Put your name on the list and give me your permission slips."

After Andrew handed him two documents, the coach nodded and told him to pick up his gear in the locker room.

Andrew could not believe all the new football equipment. The locker room floor was filled with football pads, pants, and helmets. In the shower room, he saw new football shoes, all organized by size. He stood in awe.

"Andy, make sure you get a good pair of shoes and a helmet," said the equipment coach in a friendly manner. "Then get your pants and pads. What position do you play?"

"Halfback," said Andrew.

"Do you want low or high tops?"

"Low."

"Low cuts are in the left corner of the shower," said the equipment coach, pointing to the shoes.

He then turned and yelled to the rest of the players.

"When you guys get all your equipment, get dressed and get out on the field. Let's move it."

The equipment coach focused again on Andrew.

"Everything okay, Andy?"

"Yes sir, thanks."

Fully dressed and leaving the locker room, Andrew caught a glimpse of himself in the full-length mirror. He stopped to admire just how good his dark skin looked in that all-white uniform.

"Oh Yeah," he said quietly out loud.

****

On the football field, Coach Charles McClurg cocked his baseball cap and looked seriously at the 100 players anxious to star for the Powerful Pilots.

"You all should know what it's gonna take to make this team," said the Coach, a tall thin man probably pushing 50 years old. Andrew couldn't tell.

"You start by working hard every minute, focus on your position, dedicate yourself, and put your heart into the practices," Coach McClurg continued. "You must prove to every coach here that you not only have talent and potential but are also a team player. Let's get to work."

Andrew stood with players on each side of him, all eyes on the coach, all listening intently. It was time to impress.

"Buck, take the defense," said Coach Mac. "Halfbacks and fullbacks go with Coach Brown. Offensive linemen stay here."

Gaines

****

Coach McClurg reached into his pocket and took out several note cards. Every practice was highly organized, every detail covered, every coach on top of what they were doing and what needed to be done. And not once, at least within hearing distance, did anyone make a racial slur.

Andrew loved the hard work, the team camaraderie, the chance to prove his greatness. And even though he was only 140 pounds, he shined at every opportunity during those first two weeks of practice.

He may have been running with the third string, but he was first in the wind sprints, notched blistering runs and scored numerous touchdowns. He also handled the hardest hits, and sometimes the cheapest shots.

During a one-on-one tackling drill, Matt Crawford —Andrew's nemesis from the baseball incident—cut in front of a defensive player for the chance to tackle Andrew. Crawford left early and nailed Andrew with a powerful hit that brought groans and cheers from the other players. Andrew did not even wince; he simply got up and jogged back to the line.

Coach McClurg must have realized Andrew's talent but did not address him directly. Sportswriters, however, were certainly paying notice. *The Virginian-Pilot* reported that a "Negro" was actually trying out for Norview's team, keeping daily tabs on Andrew's progress.

The final cut would be made after a preseason scrimmage against Annandale High School, a powerhouse from Northern Virginia. To Andrew's mind, it was simple—just give him the ball and he'd make the team, racial prejudice had nothing to do with football.

Heidelberg

****

Lawrence Sears was a neighbor who worked with Kenny Heidelberg Sr. at the Norfolk Naval Shipyard. It was good work that both enjoyed with a pay scale that was just below decent.

Mostly, however, Sears was known as the head football coach of the Colts in the Norfolk Recreation League. Coach Sears knew that Andrew would probably lead his team to another senior league title, but he was too much of a fan to fault his star halfback for wanting to play with Norview.

The day before the Annandale scrimmage, Coach Sears, his trademark unlit cigarette hanging from his mouth, walked across the street to visit the Heidelberg family.

"I just stopped over to see how my best halfback was doing up there with them white people," he said when Andrew's father opened the door. "I sho do miss him out dere on da field."

"Yeah, I know," said Mr. Heidelberg, "but I think he sho likes bein out dere with Norview."

Coach Sears was carrying a newspaper he had opened to the sports section.

"You see the newspaper, Kenny? Looka here at dis headline."

COLORED HALFBACK TRIES OUT FOR NORVIEW

"And he's gon make that team, too," said the proud father as his wife entered the living room from the kitchen.

"Hey, Lawrence Edward," said Mrs. Heidelberg. "I don't have any rolls today, but I know you came over to talk football."

"You know me, Lena. I'm checkin on my halfback. Dat boy is rockin da world already."

Hearing the chatter, Andrew came out of his bedroom.

"Hey, Coach."

"I know you runnin them white boys to death up dere, ain't cha?" said Sears. "Any time dey write about somebody for even tryin out for a team, dat's a story."

Coach Sears smiled, chewed on the cigarette he had in the side of his mouth, and poked Andrew in his ribs.

"Boy," he continued, "I don't know how you gon make da team if you keep losin weight."

"I don't see how he's losing weight," said Mrs. Heidelberg, "all that food he's been eating. Lil Kenny in the Army, and we still buyin the same amount of food."

"Gotta feed him, Lena," said Coach Sears as he slapped his open hand on Andrew's back. "Them some big white boys poundin on him."

Andrew stood straight from the friendly, but powerful hit.

"You gon make dat team, boy?" said Coach Sears.

"I should, Coach. I been gettin away most of the time. We got a scrimmage wit a high school from Northern Virginia tomorrow, and then I'll find out."

"Oh, you gon make it," said Coach Sears. "I'm pullin for ya."

"Thanks, Coach. Bobby tol me da Colts are lookin pretty good."

"Yeah, you know we much better wit you out dere. But I'm okay wit dat so long as I can come up to dat big stadium and watch you run all over dat field."

Andrew smiled, keeping his distance to avoid another back slap.

****

In the scrimmage against Annandale, Andrew showed his prowess with several long and impressive touchdown runs. On the sideline, Coach McClurg remained stoic.

"That boy can run," said Coach Mac to his assistant, Buck Moody.

"What's that, Mac, about the third or fourth touchdown?" said Moody. "And that's with third-string blocking. Heidelberg can fly."

Coach McClurg did not seem to be listening as he looked at the field, then yelled to the players on the sideline.

"First string, back in for 10 plays."

As Andrew and the other substitutes returned to the bench, McClurg did not congratulate anyone, keeping his focus on the field.

****

As advertised, the decision would be immediate. After the game, Andrew stood at a bulletin board in the locker room, his finger going down the list of halfbacks still on the team. His concern turned to desperation as he looked for his name ... that did not seem to be included on the list. Was there a mistake? He looked harder, but it was not there. He backed away, staring at the board in disbelief as two players walked up from behind.

"Wow, Andy, *you* got cut?" said the first. "Man, that's a tough break."

"Yeah, Andy," said the second, "I'm sorry to see that. You were good."

Andrew lowered his head and quickly left school. The walk home was a blur, tears mixed with anger, his mind racing in stunned fury. What did he have to do? Why couldn't God have stepped in and declared that this was not fair? Football was supposed to be judged on talent and heart. There was no way he wasn't good enough to make that team. He just wasn't white.

Andrew tried to yell at God, but his voice could not break through the tears crushing his soul. He walked, he ran, he cried.

****

Andrew tried to dry his face before entering his home. His mother was in the kitchen cooking dinner.

"Hello, my son," she said with a smile. "Did you have a good game?"

As mothers do, she immediately realized there was a problem.

"What's wrong, Andrew?"

He did not make eye contact, but headed toward his room, trying not to cry.

"Nothin, just tired," he said as he closed his bedroom door.

****

From within his room, Andrew was awakened by the voices of his parents and Coach Sears in the living room. The adults were agitated and angry. Andrew opened his eyes but did not leave his bed.

"I can't believe it," he heard Coach Sears say in anger. "It's terrible. You know he should be on dat team. Hell, he should be startin."

"I feel like goin up there right now and shootin eery one of them racist coaches," said Mr. Heidelberg.

"Don't say that, Kenny," his wife interrupted.

"Well, I do. That's my son, Lena, and it ain't right. Just ain't right."

"I feel so bad for Andrew," said Coach Sears. "He worked so hard and did so well. Dis meant so damn much ta him."

Andrew pulled the pillow over his head and returned to sleep.

Heidelberg

****

The following morning, *The Virginian-Pilot* ran a short and precise one-column article on the second page of its sports section with an awkwardly large headline.

NEGRO AMONG THOSE CUT AT NORVIEW
NORFOLK – The first Negro to try out for a varsity sport at any of the city's three integrated high schools was cut Friday from the Norview football squad. He is Andrew Heidelberg, a 16-year-old junior. Heidelberg was one of 10 players dropped by Coach Charles McClurg.

****

In September 1961, Andrew entered his third year of torture at Norview High School. Bobby had told him long ago that eventually the white kids would get used to him. Knuck was only partially correct. While they had slowly gotten accustomed to Andrew's invasion of their world, they had not eased the crap they continually poured on him.

Sitting in his English Literature class—third row next to the window with empty seats to the front, back, and right—Andrew pretended to be reading a book until the teacher arrived. The room was about half-full with students, most of them chatting loudly.

Andrew ignored the trivialities of the white world as he stared at a small photo of Betty Jean he had placed inside the sleeve of his book. Tommy, an irritating kid who sat in the rear of the classroom with a bunch of other idiots, motioned for his friends to be quiet as he pointed his attention to Andrew.

"Hey, Andy, did you really think you were good enough to play on a real football team?" said Tommy in a voice loud enough so that everyone in the room could hear.

Most of the students stopped to look at Andrew as the boys in the back chuckled.

"So, Andy," he continued before being interrupted by one of the girls sitting in the front row.

"Tommy, why don't you cut it out?" she said with a trace of disgust.

Obviously irritated by her remark, Tommy quickly fired back, now talking even louder.

"Don't tell me you got a crush on this here colored boy? Are you a nigger lover? Huh? Nig-uh, lov-uh?"

He paused to make a point.

"You know what happens to nigger lovers?"

Embarrassed, the girl turned back around and did not say another word. At the same time, Tommy moved toward Andrew, who had turned his head away from the room and was looking out the window, once again pretending not to hear, or care.

"So, Andy, I bet you really like da white girls, don't cha?"

Tommy suddenly stopped, his eyes noticing a small photo in the fold of Andrew's open book.

"Whoa, dude, what's this?" he added as he grabbed the picture, took a quick look, and raised it for the class.

As Andrew tried to swipe back the small picture, Tommy pulled it away to look again.

"Hey, Andrew has a girlfriend," he giggled. "She ain't white."

Andrew angrily stood up from his desk and moved toward Tommy, who was making a stupid face to depict ugliness.

"He probably thinks she's pretty," bellowed Tommy.

Andrew finally grabbed the photo out of Tommy's hand and pulled back, his piercing eyes staring at the white student.

"Settle down, Andy," said Tommy, "you sure are touchy for a

boy in love. Why don't you share your girlfriend with everyone?"

Andrew sat back down as Tommy returned to the back of the room.

"He's a lover, but he sure ain't no football player," Tommy proclaimed.

Andrew put the small, treasured photo back into his pocket and looked out the window.

****

Andrew and Bobby were sitting on the curb in front of BeLo Super Market, looking out onto Sewells Point Road.

"Bird, you really ran dat ball tonight," said Bobby. "I was even proud of you."

"Thanks, Knuck."

"I know you really wanted ta play for Norview, but it's good ta have you back on da Colts," Bobby said quietly. "Dem white boys cain't appreciate you, anyway."

Andrew silently stared into the street.

"Oh Lord, what's wrong now?" said Bobby as he tried to look into Andrew's eyes. "You and Betty Jean have a fight?"

"No, man," said Andrew. "Me and Jean are alright. Why do you always think something is wrong with me and my girl?"

"If you ain't laughing and talking about yoself, sumpin gotta be wrong wit cha," said Bobby. "And, usually, Betty Jean somewhere in da middle of it."

"No, I'm just thinking about a lot of things," Andrew said before Bobby broke into his train of thought.

"Scuse me, Bird, but yo soundin like dem crackers again."

"Sorry, Knuck, I forget where I am sometimes."

"Hey, Saturday night, Booga T playin Norcom," Bobby said excitedly. "We oughta go and see Freddy run dat ball."

144

"Yeah, I wanna see him play," said Andrew, easily joining Bobby's enthusiasm. "I know he good. Uma go. I mean um gon ask my daddy can I go."

****

As always, Booker T. Washington's old and rickety football stadium was packed, its poorly lit and dark ambiance in stark contrast to the bright stadium at Norview.

But there was great excitement and noise from the all-Black crowd of about 4,000 people in the stands and along the fences. The two competing bands were blasting music to the rhythm of bass drums as cheerleaders moved to the beat and two bitter rivals—Booker T and visiting Norcom—played quality high school ball despite wearing uniforms, pads, and helmets that seemed almost antiquated.

Standing along the fence near the end zone, Andrew and Bobby chatted loudly as the maroon and gray Bookers drove toward the goal with Freddy breaking several powerful runs, then bursting off tackle for a seven-yard touchdown as the home side rejoiced, Andrew and Bobby pounding each other on the shoulders as they danced gleefully.

For one glorious moment, Andrew had no thoughts of the white school on the other side of town.

****

If the Booker T. Washington and Norcom uniforms were shabby, they were crisp and fashionable compared to the two sets that were continuously shared in the Norfolk Recreation League. Standing on the sideline toward the end of another Colts victory, Andrew and Bobby were approached by Coach Sears.

145

Great game guys," said the coach, his unlit cigarette dangling from his mouth. "It dey don't score 35 points in da next two minutes you guys can rest up for da championship next week."

As Coach Sears paced the sidelines, Andrew looked at Bobby.

"Knuck, I been thinkin. I didn't get cut from Norview cause I wasn't good enough."

"Errybody know dat, Bird. Mosta white people too dumb ta know da difference, but all yo friends know. And I bet dem white coaches and da players up dere know dey shoulda kept you on da team."

"Yeah, Knuck, I ain't gon let dat crap get in my head. I got one mo year, too."

"Booga T needs ya, boy," said Bobby.

"Tell dat to my mamma and daddy."

"Bird, but you could be a star at Booga T."

"Knuck, I could be a star at Norview."

"Yeah, man," said Bobby, "ain't no doubt."

****

Coach Jim Brown was sitting at a makeshift registration table in the Norview gym. Not to be mistaken for the great running back for the Cleveland Browns, Norview's Brown was short and white, a graduate of Duke University in his mid-30s. Aside from being one of the school's PE teachers, he was the varsity basketball coach and the backfield coach for the football team.

Although Coach Brown had always been courteous, Andrew was not certain what role he had taken in the football cuts. Whatever, Andrew had never held him responsible.

Brown was also in charge of the intramural program.

"Coach Brown," said Andrew, "I was told to see you about signing up for intramural sports."

146

"It starts Thursday afternoon, Andy," said Brown with a smile. "It'll run for about two months. You know how it works?"

"Yes, Sir. They have horseshoes, table tennis, track ... all that stuff. And, if I win and get enough points, I get a Norview letter, am I right?"

"Yes, sir," said the coach, "all you need is 21 points."

"And I can put that "N" on one of those white Norview sweaters?"

"If you want," said Brown. "That's what the kids usually do."

That was exactly what Andrew intended to do.

Once the games began, Andrew quickly realized he had little competition. The participants were mostly students who played no varsity or JV sports. There were a few good athletes, but Andrew was the only one approaching greatness. He showed no mercy. From horseshoes to track, he dominated.

On March 19, 1960, Cal Jacox of the *Norfolk Journal and Guide*—the Tidewater area's weekly Black newspaper—printed full details of Andrew's intramural feats.

> *One of the top intramural athletes at Norview High School is Andrew Heidelberg, who is also one of the leading performers in the Norfolk Recreation Bureau's community leagues. Heidelberg holds the record for the indoor 220-yard dash. He also won the 110-yard dash and the broad jump, along with the table tennis and horseshoe crowns.*

Even many of the varsity athletes stopped by to watch the track events in the gym, perhaps to marvel at Andrew's speed and agility, perhaps to wonder what might have happened had he made the football team.

Earning 21 points was a breeze; the big blue N and the beautiful white sweater were his.

Heidelberg

****

Andrew walked through the main entrance of the school, wearing his brand new Norview letterman's sweater. The jocks assembled at the entrance looked a bit shocked and somewhat amused.

"Andy Heidelberg, you're looking good," said one Jock. "I like your sweater."

"King of the intramurals," said another. "I hear he's one mean ping pong player."

"I heard he kicked ass in horseshoes," added a third jock as everyone laughed.

Andrew usually walked past the group, acting as if he was not paying attention. Not today.

"You gentlemen are welcome to challenge me at any sport, any time," said Andrew to the group.

Silence.

"Okay, you're on," said one of the jocks. "Just as long as it's not running."

The group, including Andrew, all laughed.

Down the hall, the reception from a group of freshman boys was not as congenial.

"Hey, the nigger stole himself a sweater," giggled one of the ninth graders.

"Better take that off, boy," said a second kid. "Those are for real athletes."

As the white boys laughed, Andrew looked straight ahead. He no longer cared for their stupidity.

****

Bobby was sitting on the Heidelberg's front steps as Andrew approached from school, carrying several books, and wearing his letterman's sweater.

"Whoa, Bird, lookatchu," said Bobby, immediately standing in wonder and kidding. "I guessin dat big blue "N" doen stand for nigga."

"I ain't so sure," snapped Andrew.

"What's wrong, Bird?"

"Man, dem whiteys are sumpin else," said Andrew, his eyes fired with anger. "I win errthing in intramurals and then what happens? I find out today dat dey had da citywide intramural championship between Norview, Granby, and Maury; and they let the white guys that I beat represent Norview instead of me. Some of em even won a city championship trophy. Nobody ever even tol me bout no city championship. Let's just not invite da nigger."

Bobby could only offer sympathy.

"It ain't never gon end, Bird, you know dat."

"Knuck, dey didn't even tell me bout it."

****

For the one millionth time, Andrew had reached the breaking point. He hated whites. He somehow needed revenge, to fight back.

And so he ran, trained, relentlessly worked himself into prime condition over the long summer before his senior year. He was quicker and stronger, an animal at 150 pounds.

****

On a late summer evening, Andrew and Betty Jean were sitting on the front steps of her home as *Will You Still Love Me Tomorrow* by The Shirelles played on the radio. Within 24 hours, she would be on her way to Virginia State College in Petersburg.

"Stop looking so glum, Andrew," said Betty Jean as she playfully clipped his chin.

"Can't help it, baby. You'll be a million miles away in college. How many girls at Virginia State will have a boyfriend in high school?"

"First of all, I'll only be 75 miles away. And second, I don't care about any of that. I love you, Andrew, so stop acting like I'm leaving you for good."

"I'm really gonna miss your beautiful face, Jean. I love you so much it still makes my heart turn flips when I see you. What am I gonna do without you?"

Andrew tried to stretch his pitiful pout.

"For one thing," said Betty Jean, "you'll be too busy with school and coaching that little football team of yours."

"Shoot, Jean, the Colts ain't no little boys," said Andrew, who had agreed to coach the junior club. "They're 14 and 15 years old. But I don't know what you're talking about. I'll still miss you."

Betty Jean touched Andrew's cheek, rubbing it softly.

"Why don't you stop now?" she said softly. "You know I'll always love you. Remember? You touched the soft spot."

Betty Jean leaned close to Andrew, giving him a long and romantic kiss before slowly pulling back.

"I gotta go, Andrew. Ma Dear is on me to finish packing. I'll call you later tonight, okay?"

She gave him another kiss, this time much quicker.

"I love you," she said reassuringly.

"Yeah, me too," he said.

Andrew stood, and Betty Jean looked surprised.

Gaines

"Hey, Andrew Heidelberg, aren't you forgetting something?"

"I love you, Jean. You know that."

"I know," she said. "I just like to hear it."

Chapter 16

August 21, 1961

*I*t was a scorching Monday in late August when Andrew once again walked into the football locker room at Norview High School. Everything looked the same as the previous year—the practice uniforms and equipment lined the walls; the shoes were stacked in the shower. The equipment coach had set up a registration table.

"I thought I'd try it one more time," said Andrew.

"Well, you know the routine," replied the coach. "Give me your permission slips and go pick up your equipment."

****

Stronger and faster than the year before, Andrew moved with ease through every drill during the grueling two-a-day practices, showing brilliance both offensively and defensively. Coach McClurg noticed, as did the many white fans watching from the stands. The practices and scrimmages were also attracting a huge crowd of Blacks, all standing outside the big fence surrounding Chittum Field on the Chesapeake Boulevard side. Even the roof of William Gerald's house on Sixth Street, with a good view of the stadium from a distance, had become a regular gathering spot for about a dozen young Black boys, continually cheering for Andrew.

On the third day of practice, during individual time sprints, Coach McClurg tugged on his baseball cap as senior running back Calvin Zongolowicz crossed the finish line with a strong sprint. Coach Buck Moody clicked his stopwatch and announced Zongo's time to McClurg. As the head coach jotted the result down on one of the 3x5 cards he carried in his back pocket, Moody signaled Coach Brown at the starting line.

"Heidelberg, you're up," said Brown.

Andrew heard several players chattering encouragement as he stepped to the line, his mind and body focused. At Brown's whistle, Andrew pushed with stinging power and flew down the course, passing the finish line to the wild cheers of teammates. Moody looked twice at his stopwatch before showing it to McClurg, who moved his cap back and smiled.

"Buck, let's move Heidelberg to safety and let him run with the first team," said McClurg.

"Good idea," said Moody. "Any change for offense?"

"Keep him running with the second string," said McClurg, "but put him deep for returns. Let's see what he can do."

What he could do was impressive—from quick and fearless defensive coverage to dazzling kickoff and punt returns.

At the end of practice that day, as the players headed for the locker room, Zongolowicz caught up to Andrew and walked beside him.

"Nice job, Andy," said Zongo.

Andrew had never spoken to C.J. but knew his reputation as one of Norview's best running backs.

"Thanks," said Andrew.

153

Zongo pounded on Andrew's shoulder pad.

"Man, where'd you get those moves?"

****

During an afternoon intra-squad scrimmage, Andrew caught a short pass from second-string quarterback Donald Strickland, then bolted past several defenders to earn big yardage. As he returned to the sideline, the roar of Black fans could be distinctly heard.

"Run dat ball, Bird," yelled one of the kids darting back-and-forth outside the fence.

He could also hear the shouts coming from atop William Gerald's house.

"You da man, Bird," yelled one of his fans from Chesapeake Manor.

As Andrew stood on the sideline, Strickland and lineman David Fitzgerald walked up to him.

"Good job, Andy," said Fitzgerald.

"You sure got a lot of friends out there," added Strickland.

"You got a lot in here too," said Fitzgerald. "Just keep it up, man. They gotta let you play this year."

Andrew smiled, shaking his head up and down to acknowledge the compliments. The moment was interrupted by a yell from Coach McClurg, commanding everyone's attention.

"Coaches, bring em in," bellowed McClurg.

Gathering to a large huddle, the teammates shouted and clapped as if getting ready to play a real game. Team captains' Ken Whitley and John Hughes, along with Zongo, were in the middle of the pack.

"Come on guys, let's put it to em," yelled Whitley, the returning

All-State first-team fullback and heavyweight wrestling champion.

"Yeah, everybody, let's go," chimed Hughes, Norview's other returning All-State star. He was bigger than the compact Whitley and considered just as tough.

"Act like you wanna hurt somebody, damn it," added Zongo, who was not a captain, but as the oldest player on the team, a natural leader.

The noise from the Pilots was deafening as everyone—including Andrew—clapped, pounded, and screamed.

"Okay, okay, that's enough, listen up, fellas," said McClurg, obviously pleased with the spirit. "You sound like you're not tired."

The noise intensified.

"We're not tired," said Whitley. "Nobody here is tired."

Instinctively, the team began to chant, "Norview, Norview, Norview … louder and louder.

Coach Moody tried to yell above the bedlam.

"Let them run some more, Coach?" he asked McClurg, who raised his hands for quiet.

"Alright, let's save it for tomorrow's scrimmage," said McClurg, as the players quieted. "I want to remind you that Highland Springs is a good football team, and we're going to introduce them to Eastern District football."

Again, the noise as 100 players yelled in agreement. Again, McClurg raised his arms for silence.

"One more thing," said Coach Mac. "Tomorrow will be the last scrimmage, and then we're gonna reduce the varsity squad to 45 players. Now, some of you younger players will be going over to the JV team, and some of you won't make either team. Let's see who's ready to play some football."

Heidelberg

****

Andrew did not care whether the Highland Springs Springers, from the suburbs of Richmond, were mighty or weak. He only wanted to erase the thoughts of a season past, that he would once again be punished for not being white. Before taking the field, Zongo and Fitzgerald had both walked by his locker and patted him on the shoulder as if they sensed his anguish.

Taking a deep breath as he left the locker room, Andrew was greeted immediately by an array of shouts and applause from several hundred Black people clustered at the fence.

"What's up fellas?" he said quietly, almost embarrassed, as he started into a light jog, still waving his hand to acknowledge those who called his name.

****

As the coaches shouted last-minute instruction and encouragement, the Norview team was massed on the sideline, loose and ready for battle. There was an excited roar in the bleachers as well as the Chesapeake Boulevard fence, where the huge throng of Black fans maneuvered for the best view.

Andrew was standing near Coach Moody.

"We want some hard-nosed football today," yelled Moody. "If you don't want none, get back."

Moody noticed Andrew and moved square to the front of his face.

"Andy, if you want some, son," he said, "get in there and get it."

"Yes sir, Coach, I want some," replied Andrew, looking directly into Moody's eyes.

The coach tightened his fist and hit Andrew on the shoulder.

"Thata boy, son, let's play some football," he said while

walking away.

"Huddle up," roared Coach McClurg as the entire team quickly moved toward him.

"Here's how it works," commanded McClurg. "They'll run 10 plays, then we run 10 plays. We keep doing that until they've had enough. Understand?"

"Yes sir," the team responded.

"Hold nothing back," added McClurg. "Keep your eyes open, use your speed, your power, your heart. This is our time, our field, our moment. Make it count. Are you ready?"

Again, the entire team shouted "yes sir" in unison.

"First-team defense," yelled McClurg, "take the field."

Andrew strapped his helmet and ran to the 40 with the rest of the starting defense. There were loud cheers from all sections of the stadium. Near midfield, the Pilots huddled around Whitley, who would play both ways—fullback and middle linebacker.

"Okay boys, 6-3, crush em," Whitley growled.

No problem.

Running off tackle, the Highland Springs halfback was met hard at the line of scrimmage, followed by three more attempts without yardage. On their fifth offensive play, one of the Springer halfbacks shot through a momentary hole, only to be leveled by Whitley.

Andrew had yet to scuff his uniform.

"That's five straight runs," said Whitley in the Norview defensive huddle. "They're gonna throw pretty soon. Let's go 5-4. Eyes open. Hit em hard."

Sure enough, the Highland Springs quarterback scrambled as Andrew shadowed one of their wide receivers. Under duress, the QB eventually dumped a short pass over the middle to the tight end, met sharply by Whitley, the ball skirting to the ground. On the last play of the series, the visitors went deep only to have the ball batted away by Andrew.

As the defense headed to the sideline, Whitley was slow getting up and needed to be helped by the trainer. Coach McClurg, seeing his all-state weapon limping back to the sideline, turned in Andrew's direction.

"Heidelberg," he shouted.

Andrew moved quickly to the head coach.

"Yes sir."

"Andy, get in there at halfback and tell Crawford to move to fullback," said McClurg.

"Yes sir, Coach," Andrew said as he strapped on his helmet and darted back onto the field.

"All right, Andy," he heard Coach Brown shouting. "Let's go."

As Andrew reached the huddle, Norview senior quarterback Harry Wilkerson stood with his back to the ball while facing his team, linemen in front and backs in the rear, his eyes moving from player to player.

"Okay, I wanna see some blocking in here," said Wilkerson, whose eyes now focused on Andrew.

"Andy, let's get it going," he said. "Give me strong right, dive right on two. Read-eee break ..."

"Break," said the other 10 offensive players in unison with the quarterback.

As the team broke huddle, John Hughes turned to Andrew. "Follow me, 33."

Andrew lined up directly behind Hughes and focused on the right tackle's butt.

Wilkerson took the snap, turned to his right, and handed the ball quickly to number 33. Smoothly swallowing the hand off, Andrew ran straight for Hughes' rear as his lineman drove the defensive tackle into the ground. Andrew cut sharply to the right, took two quick steps, cut back left, and headed down the sideline, racing 60 yards without being touched as Norview's players and the crowd of fans outside the fence went wild. As for the white fans in the stands, the excitement was blended with a dose of disbelief.

"Did you see that?" yelled one of the white students to a group of friends still cheering Andrew's run. "Nobody even touched him. That's unbelievable."

A second white boy, a brash smile on his face, spoke even louder.

"Yeah, that nigger looked like he was chasin a chicken dinner," he giggled.

As the white kid waited for laughter, he was surprised that his friends acted as if they didn't hear him, the girl to his right looking away in partial disgust.

"Man, that Andy is good," said the first white boy as the group continued to yell their excitement to the field.

The white boy who made the racist remark looked again at his friends, then cupped his hands around his mouth and joined the cheers.

"Let's go, Pilots," he yelled. "Do it again."

****

The Norview locker room approached bedlam, the sound of football cleats walking on the tile floor etched in crazy harmony with the noise and excitement from the players.

Andrew sat at his locker, still wearing his uniform, many walking by to pound him on the shoulder pad. Andrew smiled appreciatively at each congratulatory remark. Certainly, he had been the star of the scrimmage, hadn't he? Certainly, he had done enough, hadn't he?

As Andrew opened his locker door, Zongo sat down on the

bench beside him, putting his arm around Andrew's shoulder.

"Andy, way to run that ball," said Zongo. "What'd you score? Seven touchdowns?"

"I'on know, man," said Andrew with a sheepish smile. "I wasn't counting."

"I know you got a lot more than me today," Zongo kidded. "What you trying to do, take over the team or something?"

"Not me, I'm just trying to stay beside you," Andrew said. "I think we look good running together."

Zongo shook his head in agreement.

"Yeah, I guess we do at that," he said. "But you're the guy whose gonna be the talk of the town."

"Well, Zongo, I think I already am," said Andrew with a sly grin.

With another pound on the shoulder pads, Zongo got up to leave.

"Anyway," he said, "I figure you got plenty more of them touchdowns, buddy."

"I hope so," Andrew said quietly.

****

The locker room was near empty as Andrew apprehensively approached the bulletin board to check the cut list. His fingers were shaking as he looked over the final roster, his eyes stopping at "running backs." He slowly read the names—Whitley, Zongolowicz, Heidelberg. His heart pounded, leaving the other names on the list a mere blur.

Andrew wiped his forehead, his smile so wide it hurt, his body fighting against his out-of-control breath. He pulled slightly back, his eyes filling with tears. He had to look again, saw his name, and the words came out loud.

"Yes! Yes!"

As Andrew turned around in pure glee, three players were standing behind him—Whitley, Hughes, and Zongolowicz. Smiling, they held out their hands to shake.

"Welcome to the Norview Pilots, Andy," said Whitley.

Andrew could hardly speak but had no way of hiding his happiness.

"Oh yeah," he said as the three team leaders shook his hand and pounded on his shoulders.

****

Andrew was walking along the long school fence at Sewells Point Road, pretending to play football and talking out loud to himself.

"Strong right, dive right on two. Read-eee break! Ready, set, hut 1, hut 2, hut 3 ..."

Momentarily imagining he was the quarterback, he handed the ball off to himself, then dodged left and right, now sounding as if he was broadcasting the game ...

"Ladies and gentlemen, Andrew Heidelberg is gone again. Touchdown Norview. The crowd goes wild. The Bird can't be stopped as the Pilots bury Granby. Wake up, y'all. We ain't never seen a halfback wit moves like this. Not Jim Brown, not Lenny Moore, not even Ollie Matson. Did you hear that? He's better than Ollie Matson? He's the best in years, maybe the best there ever was ..."

****

The party in the Heidelberg home just sort of erupted. Coach Sears, his unlit cigarette hanging from his lips, ecstatically congratulated Andrew while friends filled the living room with noise and laughter.

"Here's my boy," he proudly proclaimed to everyone. "Hey, Lenny Moore, you ready for the big leagues?"

Coach Sears followed with a bear hug and a two-handed shoulder shake, then stepped back with the mightiest of smiles while chewing on that cigarette.

"I know you gon score two touchdowns in dat first game, ain't cha?"

"If dey give me a chance to run," said Andrew.

"They better," bellowed Coach Sears, "or me and Kenny'll be down on that field so fast."

He looked at Mr. Heidelberg, who had been carrying the same huge smile since he heard the news.

"Huh, Kenny?" grunted Coach Sears.

"That's right, Sears," said Mr. Heidelberg. "Hey, Lena, my son plays for Norview. My son plays for Norview."

Mr. Heidelberg pulled Coach Sears to within whispering distance but did not whisper.

"We better get seats on the 50-yard line," he bellowed.

Everyone in the room heard the remark, breaking out into louder laughter and setting off another round of gracious hugs, Andrew's mother fighting off everyone for the longest grasp.

Mr. Heidelberg looked at Andrew, his grin finally turning serious. "Don't matter where we sit, Son, we gon be cheerin."

"You got that right, Kenny," Mrs. Heidelberg interrupted, once again hugging her son, this time even tighter, her voice progressing from happiness to joyful tears to outright crying.

"Andrew, Andrew, Andrew ... my son."

Chapter 17

Senior Year

As Andrew approached Norview on the first day of school, two thoughts buzzed within his brain—he was a senior, and he was on the football team. What took over, however, was history ...this place had not been kind to him.

As if by instinct, he tensed as he walked through Norview's front door and into the main hallway. No need.

"How you doin, Andy?" said one of the guys gathered at their jock hangout just inside the entrance.

"Andy Heidelberg, star running back," announced John Hughes.

"Hey, Andy," said another.

"What the hell?" thought Andrew as he greeted the athletes with a smile and slight hand wave but kept walking just the same.

Into the hallway, many of the kids looked at him, but there were no taunts or racial slurs. One male student, who was walking and talking to a female friend, nearly ran into Andrew.

"Oh, hey," he said almost apologetically for the collision. "Andy, I heard you made the football team. Congratulations."

"Wow, that's really cool," said the girl. "It must be exciting."

"Yeah, sure is," answered Andrew, his guard fading fast.

"Oh, well, good luck, Andy," said the girl.

"Thanks," said Andrew as he continued to class, kind greetings from others as well.

The entire day, not one person called him a nigger. It was almost eerie.

****

Two days before Norview's opening game, the home stands at Chittum Field were packed with students and teachers—players and coaches at midfield as the cheerleaders turned the crowd into a frenzy with the "Gimme N-O-R-V-I-E-W" routine. Andrew, wearing jersey number 33 over his school clothes stood with the other running backs as Coach McClurg promised yet another extraordinary season. It was a beautiful display of massive adoration.

Andrew Heidelberg had arrived.

****

Friday, September 22, 1961—game day. George Graves, a rather proper and boring teacher who probably did not attend football games, was lecturing about world history. Evidently, the French peasants discovered a unique way of dealing with greed.

Sitting in the back of the classroom, listening to the monotone lecture, Andrew was surrounded by white students seated in the desks to his side, front, and back.

After a knock on the door, a cheerleader entered the classroom. She was wearing a white sweater with a big blue N in the middle, a blue pleated skirt, and white socks with blue and white saddle shoes. Everyone, including Mr. Graves, listened as she began to talk.

"Hi, ya'll. I want to wish Andy Heidelberg good luck tonight against Princess Anne."

Nearly everyone in the class turned toward Andrew with an immediate, seemingly heartfelt, burst of cheers and applause. Several students even hooted as a few more offered comments about hammering Princess Anne.

The cheerleader, who was beautiful, approached Andrew, still seated at his desk. The once noisy classroom quieted as she pinned a blue paper football on his shirt. She then bent down to give Andrew a kiss on his cheek ...

"Good luck tonight, Andy. Beat Princess Anne."

As she turned to leave, the classroom was once again filled with applause and encouragement. Sure, a couple of the male students looked away or glared, but there were no derogatory remarks or gasps of shock. Even bland old Mr. Graves smiled before returning to his script.

Andrew did not process another word he said.

****

Amidst the noisy crowd of players getting dressed for the game, Andrew sat at his locker, wearing his "game face" and brand-new uniform—white jersey with the blue bars across the shoulders and number 33 stretching clear across his chest. The pants were crispy white with a red and blue stripe along each leg. The long white, knee socks had a two-inch-wide red band at the top, trimmed with thin blue stripes above and below it. Short white socks were worn on top of them. Andrew's black cleats were shined to a sparkle.

He carefully wrapped white tape on each wrist, his black skin looking radiant against all the white.

Heidelberg

Coach Moody approached, reading his game notes, probably not appreciating just how stunning Andrew looked.

"Heidelberg, let's make sure we're all on the same page," Moody said in a voice that was obviously focused on business.

Andrew stood up, his helmet in hand.

"Yes sir, Coach."

"Starting right halfback, starting defensive safety, and deep back on punt and kickoff returns," said Moody. "Got it?"

"Yes sir, Coach."

Moody looked closely into Andrew's eyes.

"You need a breather, you let us know."

Moody's face developed a silly grin.

"But you're probably not gonna need any breather, are you, 33?"

Andrew smiled.

"Not tonight, Coach."

Coach Moody moved even closer.

"You want some, son?" he said in a quiet, commanding voice.

Looking directly into Coach Moody's eyes, Andrew did not hesitate with his answer.

"I want some, Coach."

"Then you get in there and get it," the coach roared.

"Yes sir, Coach."

"Thata boy," said Moody as he headed for another player.

Andrew surveyed the raucous locker room, watching Whitley and Hughes move to the center of the madness as if preparing for war.

"All right, guys, let's get ready to go," yelled Whitley.

The team immediately closed in around the two captains.

"I heard some garbage about this bein their second game, as if that's gonna matter," bellowed Whitley. "Let's hit em hard and let em know we came to play football!"

The team responded, Andrew making as much noise as anyone. Zongo paced through the crowd, pounding players on their shoulder pads. Just as Zongo neared, Whitley was already nose-to-nose with Andrew.

"You better run that damn ball tonight, Andy," growled Whitley.

"Okay," Andrew responded as Zongo grabbed his arm and yanked him away.

"You can do it, Andy," said Zongo. "And don't worry about a thing. Ain't nobody gonna mess with you as long as I'm here. You got it?"

"Got it."

Whitley raised his helmet high into the air.

"Guys, when we get out there," he yelled, "everybody stops at the goal post. We line up and run on the field together, as a team."

The Powerful Pilots shouted in agreement, then walked out of the locker room amid yells and shouts from all who saw them coming, the noise of their football cleats banging against the concrete landing, down three short steps, and onto the sidewalk. The cleats muffled as the 60 players walked onto the grass near the tennis courts to line up under the goal post. Of course, now the shouting from the team itself could hardly be heard over the noise of more than 11,000 fans whose voices escalated when the cheerleaders hoisted the huge, white paper banner with "Go Pilots" written in big, blue letters.

"Ladies and Gentlemen," announced the public address announcer, "let's welcome the 1961 Norview Pilots."

Following their captains, the team burst through the huge banner and ran to the benches, the noise from the crowd now at a fever pitch. As the players jumped up and down on the sidelines, pumping one another up for the onslaught, Andrew paced the front of the Norview bench—serious, nervous, and excited. He was looking up toward the home stands when Zongo ran up beside him.

"What a night for football," Zongo said.

"Man," said Andrew, still staring at the crowd. "Seeing all these white people together under these lights, it's so bright. Looks like the sun is still shining."

And so, Andrew Heidelberg's high school football career began, Bill Piersall of WNOR reporting every moment from the radio booth.

"Heidelberg looks, as the saying goes, like a fly in a bucket of buttermilk," rambled Piersall. "And we would be remiss if we didn't mention what some folks have been wondering. Will the Norview players even care to block for Andy Heidelberg?"

"Let's break every bone in that skinny nigger's body," the Princess Anne captain told his team.

****

Andrew's eyes widened as he saw the football coming straight to him, high and spinning ...

"Heidelberg catches it at about the 19," Piersall told the radio audience. "He takes a few steps straight ahead, quickly veers outside to the right, there's blocking, he's down the sideline ... midfield, 45, 40, 35. Nobody's gonna catch him, he's untouched ... 10, 5, touchdown! Goodness, what a run, what a weapon ... 81 yards on the opening kickoff. The first time Norview's colored halfback touches the ball, unbelievable! The home crowd is going nuts. Pilots on top."

Andrew lightly deposited the ball in the end zone as bedlam ruled the stadium, from the white Norview fans in the stands and the Black Norview fans in the corner of the visitor side and outside the fence. As for the Princess Anne fans, they were stunned, some downright angry and disgusted. In the press box, a beaming Piersall was still standing, having accidentally knocked over his chair during Andrew's touchdown.

"Well, so much for the prediction that the Norview players might not block for their colored halfback," the radio announcer reported. "He's being mobbed by coaches and teammates."

On the Norview sidelines, an excited and expressive Coach Moody was talking to his defense.

"Listen, guys, we're only 20 seconds into the game. It's not over. Don't let em off the hook. Hit em hard. Four and out, got it? Don't let up."

"Yes sir," the defensive team answered.

After the kickoff, the defense huddled around Whitley.

"Remember what Coach said," barked number 48. "Nobody lets up. Smash em, 6-3, break."

Andrew and Zongo lined up at the corners, Whitley at middle linebacker. Princess Anne's first play was off tackle going for about two yards until snuffed by Whitley. Andrew had moved up close to the pile only to be heftily bumped from behind by a Princess Anne receiver well past the whistle.

"Watch it, nigger," grumbled the receiver.

Andrew turned to look at the rude aggressor, who burst directly into Andrew's face, helmet-to-helmet.

"You ain't gonna live through this game, nigger."

Two of Andrew's teammates immediately moved into the discussion, as did a referee.

"Break it up, guys," ordered the official. "Break it up."

Surrounded by Norview players, the Princess Anne player pulled away, but had another quiet word as he left, once again bumping Andrew.

"See ya, nigger."

Continuing to run interference, the referee shuffled the

Princess Anne player back to his huddle.

"Let's play football," said the ref.

After Norview made a couple of solid hits on defense, Andrew again had a meeting with the Cavalier receiver who had bumped and threatened him, number 33 diving to knock down a pass. Andrew expected more words, but the kid quietly returned to his huddle, the visitors forced to punt.

On offense, Norview was not having much luck running the ball. Whitley and Zongo had each picked up good yardage, but the drives stalled. On Norview's third offensive series, Andrew took a handoff and was hammered after a 5-yard gain. Under the pile, he was poked, harassed, and spit on by an opposing tackler, who, while getting to his feet, pushed down on Andrew before adding a slight kick.

"Scuse me, nigger," said the tackler.

As Andrew tossed the ball to the referee and put his hand into his helmet to wipe the spit from his cheek, Dave Fitzgerald grabbed his arm.

"Andy," Fitzgerald said in surprise, "Did he just call you a nigger?"

"Did he?" said Andrew. "I'on know. I was just thinkin bout how bad he smells."

Both laughed as they returned to the huddle.

Late in the second quarter—having built a 14-0 lead with a 32-yard touchdown run by Zongolowicz—Norview seemed willing to run out the clock on its own end of the field. As the Norview band assembled in the end zone for the halftime show, an 18-yard draw play by Whitley moved the ball to their own 42. There was still a minute left.

"Wilkerson fakes to Heidelberg," reported Piersall. "He goes back to pass, throws over the middle, complete to Heidelberg ... he breaks to daylight ... he is gone, just like that. Andy Heidelberg,

58-yard touchdown. He runs right into the Norview band down in the end zone. This is crazy!"

Tangled amid the horn section, Andrew was an instant hero, mauled by a line of clarinetists and an overzealous tuba player. Even the majorettes joined the mob.

In the second half, Zongo intercepted a pass and returned it 22 yards for another touchdown, Norview on its way to a 34-0 victory.

The two teams lined up to exchange words of sportsmanship, most of the Princess Anne players refusing to shake Andrew's hand. But as the players broke, Andrew was again congratulated by teammates and mobbed by many white Norview students, along with even more Black fans who had rushed the field to celebrate.

To this part of the world, it was a scene like no other.

****

Norview's locker room was pure pandemonium. Andrew was still wearing his uniform when two reporters approached his locker.

"Great game, Andy," said the first reporter. "Were you nervous out there?"

"I was so scared I was trembling," he answered, as if he had been giving interviews his entire life. "But I felt really good after that first touchdown. That kickoff return was the best feeling I've ever had in my life."

"Did you have any problems? Any dirty play?"

"Ain't nothin but dirty plays in football," said Andrew. "I just kept runnin as fast as I could every time I touched the ball."

"So, nobody said anything?" asked a reporter.

"Well," answered Andrew, "my guys were saying, 'nice

touchdown! Their guys were sorta quiet."

Both reporters laughed as Andrew smiled.

"How does it feel to be a star, Andy?"

"Good."

Good? Andrew Heidelberg was born to give interviews. He was ready to say more, but a third reporter suddenly put a tape recorder close to his face and began speaking in a serious tone.

"Andy, everybody keeps saying that you shouldn't have been cut last year. Do you think you didn't make the team because you were too light?"

"Naw," said Andrew, "I don't think I was too light. I think I was too dark."

Caught off guard by the answer, the once serious reporter broke into a huge grin. This was fun.

After the three sportswriters left and players dispersed, Cal Jacox of the area's weekly Black newspaper—*The Journal & Guide*—walked up to Andrew's locker. As always, Jacox was wearing his distinctive thin-brimmed black hat.

"Hey, Andy Heidelberg," Jacox said with the kind of smile reserved for best of friends.

"Hey, Mr. Jacox," Andrew replied, thrilled to see his favorite sports reporter.

"I must tell you," Jacox laughed, "I've never been in a white locker room before."

"Yeah, takes some gettin used to," quipped Andrew.

"I was sort of expecting somebody to tell me I couldn't be here."

"Me too," laughed Andrew. "Maybe if I keep scorin dem touchdowns, they'll let us stay."

****

Andrew was sound asleep, the clock in his bedroom reading a few minutes past 6 a.m. Not even bothering to knock, Mr. Heidelberg barreled into the room carrying a bundle of newspapers under his arm. With a huge and proud smile, he put the papers on the foot of the bed, grabbing one while waking his son.

"Andrewkie, Andrewkie," he boomed. "Look at that name in the newspaper. Look at the size of this headline. Ain't never seen no colored person's name that big in The Virginian Pilot. Boy, wake up and look. Somebody in this room is famous."
Andrew sat up in the bed and rubbed his eyes.

"Ha," bellowed his father with an exaggerated laugh, putting the newspaper directly in Andrew's face. Now awake and interested, Andrew grabbed the newspaper out of his dad's hands.

"Man, that's me," Andrew exclaimed, looked at his Dad, then back at the newspaper.

"Whoa," laughed Andrew as his mother entered the room, picking up one of the papers and shaking her head in glee.

"I can't believe my son is this famous," she boasted. "Boy, you really played some football out there last night."

"He's a Heidelberg, ain't he?" said Andrew's father.

The uncontrollable smile having never left his face, Andrew looked at his parents, then glanced down at the newspaper again. Getting out of bed, Andrew waved the newspaper and crazily chanted one of the cheerleaders' routines.

"Andy, Andy, he's our man, if he can't do it, nobody can!"

"Oh, I wish Lil Kenny could have seen the game," said Mrs. Heidelberg as the family laughed and danced. "I can't wait to send him all these articles."

Andrew calmed down, the joy turning to a dose of nostalgia.

Heidelberg

"You know," he said, "I really love Norview. It's the best school in the world."

"Goodness," said Mrs. Heidelberg as she moved to hug her son. "I never thought I would hear those words."

Chapter 18

Bird and Knuck Go Deep

L ate that afternoon, Andrew and Bobby were sitting on the bench beside the mailbox at the front corner of the Heidelberg home. Several older neighbors walked by and waved.

"Hello there, Andrew," said one, "congratulations on your great game last night."

Two young boys, about 9 or 10 years old, stopped their bicycles when they saw the football star.

"Hey, Bird, I saw yo touchdowns, both of dem. We was on top William Gerald's house at Six Stop. Dey was beautiful."

"Number 33, Bird," added the second boy, "You tore em apart, man. I hope I get ta go ta Norview someday."

"Thanks, guys," said Andrew as the boys got back on their bikes.

"See ya later, Bird," said the first kid as they peddled away.

Surveying the scene, Bobby could only shake his head.

"You member, Bird, when Johnny Morris scored 127 points in that basketball game when Norcom beat Mary N. Smith? Man, da white newspaper had a dinky paragraph on da back page."

Bobby became dramatically expressive as he painted a visual

of the Johnny Morris headline with his hand, his fingers close together to show the small size of the font.

"Negro scores 127 points. Damn, Bird, two touchdowns and you all o'er da front page."

Bobby was now on a roll as he visualized Andrew's game by opening his hand, stretching his thumb and index finger to suggest the huge headline.

"HEIDELBERG A STAR," Bobby announced to Andrew's delight.

"Oh yeah, Knuck, and they even spelled my name right."

Pulling his shoulders back, Andrew produced an extremely sly look.

"So, Knuck," he said, then waited for Bobby to answer.

"Yeah?"

"So, Knuck, did I look good?"

Bobby looked sarcastically at Andrew, mimicking the first two words for emphasis.

"So, Bird, you mean good lookin or good playin?"

"Knuck, I know I'm good lookin, especially when I'm wearing Number 33 in them spankin new Norview uniforms. I even had on my white tape wristbands."

"Yeah," Bobby shot back, "I saw yo show-boatin wit dat tape all over yo wrists an shoes like you was Lenny Moore or sumpin."

Bobby paused.

"You played all right," he added.

Popping Bobby on the arm, Andrew stood up quickly from the bench in comic disbelief.

"All right? I scored two touchdowns, turkey. I was all over that field. Prince Anne ... Princess Anne couldn't stop me."

"Well, in that case," said Bobby, "I guess you looked damn good playin against dem white boys."

"What's that supposed to mean?"

176

"Just what I said. Bird, you know dem white boys cain't run like da niggas. Somebody at Booga T woulda toe yo ass up comin round dat corner."

Andrew's jaw dropped.

"So, you don't think I could have run like that against Booker T?"

"I don't think, I know," said Bobby. "Ain't no way you coulda run like that against Booga T. Errbody on Booga T can outrun dem white boys up dere and you know dat. I ain't sayin you wouldna scoed one or two times, but you wouldna been runnin like dat against Booga T. Plus, Mister Headlines, Booga T woulda kicked yo white-boy asses all ova dat field."

Andrew was now infuriated.

"Don't talk shit about my school, nigga?"

"Oh, now it's yo school? I'on even see how you say dat. Dey treat you like shit since you got dere, then you sco two touchdowns and now you in love wit da place?"

Stunned by Bobby's bluntness, Andrew had no answer ... for about 15 seconds.

"Let me tell you something, Knuck. I've thought about this a lot."

"Oh, here we go."

"I'm gonna spit it out, Knuck. I think most of the white people are okay."

"What? C'mon, nigga. Dey done wash yo brain with cat piss."

"No, seriously. I been watching them for three years. There are good whiteys and bad whiteys."

"Oh yeah, Bird, da good whiteys! Sorry, I ain nevah seen one."

"Oh, they're there. They've just been sort of hiding. They think the bad whiteys, because of all the noise they make, are in the majority."

"Whatchu, out dere takin a survey now of who gonna hang yo

ass and who gonna politely look da otha way?"

"You got that right, Knuck ... and I ain't defending the good whiteys. But there is one more thing I know I noticed ... the good whiteys are scared. They've been told that anyone who even smiles at a nigga gonna get his lips chopped off, or worse, a big 'N' carved on their forehead ... and it doesn't stand for Norview."

"I ain't buyin dis, Bird."

"No, it's true. We both know there are way too many bad whiteys out there. But the good whiteys go along with all that shit because they want to be safe."

"Dat's good, Bird. Now I get it. An I am so happy dem good whiteys are safe. Dat means so much to me."

"Yeah, Knuck, it's sad."

"Lemme ask you, Bird, how many dem white boys yo playin wit on Norview been callin you 'nigger' for the last three years?"

"Maybe just a few," said Andrew. "Couple apologized. Man, we teammates now."

"Teammates? What about friends? You got any friends up dere? I mean friends like me?"

Andrew smiled in a kidding nature.

"Ain't nobody got no friend like you, Knuck."

Bobby wasn't smiling.

"Naw, I'm serious, Bird. You got any friends?"

"Yeah, some. I know some of them don't like me, but they keep their distance. Yeah, there's some guys I'm friends with. Gets better and better."

"How many invite you to der home?"

Andrew paused.

"Nobody yet," he said, his voice now rising in frustration. "Man, this is Virginia, Knuck. We only played one game."

"Well, you tell me how it's goin by time da season ends?" said

Bobby. "I wanna see if some a dem white boys, dem teammates, gon invite you fo dinner. But, if dey do, Bird, just make sho dey taste da food first."

Bobby smiled, easing the pressure. Andrew also relaxed his mood, then looked seriously at his best friend.

"Well, let me tell you something else I've been thinking about for a while now, Knuck."

Andrew momentarily paused, as if it was important that his wording was precise.

"I look at it this way, man. Me going to the white school isn't just about integration. Because ever since I can remember, people always say that high school is supposed to be the best time in your life. Well, it ain't happened for me. All I wanna be is a regular high school kid, going to school and having a good time. I think I deserve that. In fact, I know I do."

"Oh, you deserve it, that's for sho," said Bobby. "But, Bird, you ain't never gon be no regular high school boy. Man, just look at you on da football field. You may be talkin like summa dem crackers, but you just a nigga in a white boy uniform."

Andrew's shoulders slumped ever so slightly.

"Yeah, I know, Knuck, but don't you go preaching to me."

"I ain't preachin," said Bobby. "I'm just tellin ya, don't go gettin too cocky. You better remember it's Mr. Charlie you playin wit our dere."

Andrew smiled while slowly shaking his head in agreement, running his teeth over his lip with a scraping bite.

"And, Bird, you can smile now, but I hear y'all next game in Lynchburg," added Bobby. "You know dat's Ku Klux Klan country, doncha nigga? Dat's bout 200 miles from home. You better hope E.C. Glass don't hang yo ass at halftime, nigga, if you even still alive."

"I ain't scared of them," said Andrew. "Coach says they got

a real good team, probably one of the best in the state. Some people think they might be state champs, but we are gonna kick their butt right in their own home."

"Well, just in case, keep yo teammates close by," said Bobby. "Yo butt gon be a long way from Oakwood."

Chapter 19

Glass

L ate Saturday morning, the Norview players—handsomely dressed in coats and ties—had boarded the team bus parked in front of the school, awaiting the coaches and driver. Andrew was seated next to David Fitzgerald near the middle. The first road trip ...

Suddenly, a 1956 Chevy, turquoise-and-white, pulled up and stopped, literally blocking the front door of the bus. Andrew noticed four teenage boys inside, but one got out on the passenger's side. Jumping aboard the bus, he grabbed the pole at the first row.

"Is smoke meat on this bus?" he yelled in quick, short, distinct words.

The kid immediately jumped off the bus and into the awaiting open door of the car. Its passengers hooting and screaming, the Chevy sped away with its tires squealing. On the bus, some of the players laughed and some talked quizzically, exchanging notes on what exactly had just happened. From the back of the bus, Zongo sprang from his seat and yelled angrily at the team.

"I don't see anything funny," he roared, demanding attention as he stormed to the front of the bus, where he turned in anger and looked directly at Andrew.

"Andy, don't pay any attention to that ass hole," he said, then addressed the team in fury. "Somebody find out who that kid is and let me know. When we get back, I'm gonna kick his ass."

Several of the team members immediately divulged the kid's name.

"His name is Phil something," said one of the players. "He is an asshole."

"He's in my homeroom," said another. "I'll take you right to him."

"Better yet, Zongo," said a third, "I know where he lives."

Zongo still had his back to the door as Coach McClurg and the two assistant coaches, Moody and Brown, stepped onto the bus.

"C.J., what was that all about?" said McClurg.

"Nothing, coach," said Zongo quietly. "Some idiot just jumped on the bus thinkin he was real funny by hasslin Andy."

McClurg stoically processed Zongo's explanation, not looking to see where Andrew was seated.

"I see," said the coach, "thanks."

As Zongo headed back to his seat, Coach Mac turned his attention to the players.

"Men, we've got a long bus ride," he said. "We'll stop around 4 to eat. Relax and enjoy the ride."

****

The 200-mile trip from Norfolk to Lynchburg took forever, the bus finally parking outside a restaurant near the center of the city. It was after 4 o'clock, the players somewhat lethargic by the journey and lack of food. Coach Moody told everyone to remain seated and went to see if the restaurant was ready for

45 starving football players. After a few minutes, he returned.

"Okay, guys, listen up," said Moody. "The restaurant won't be ready to feed us for another half hour. Why don't you guys get off and stretch your legs for a while. Take a short walk around town but stay together and be back at 4:30. I want to make this perfectly clear, absolutely no horseplay."

****

Ken Whitley and John Hughes led the pack of Pilots walking down the main street of Lynchburg. Seemingly deserted on a late Saturday afternoon, the center of town was rather unnerving with the old architecture and strange quiet. The team reached a large, stately building with four pillars that was obviously some sort of courthouse.

From the middle of the group, walking with Zongo and Fitzgerald, Andrew looked up at the writing on top of the building's face, reading the words softly to himself.

"Prince Edward County," he said slowly. "Why does dat ring a bell?"

Fitzgerald had the answer.

"Hey, Andy," he said, "It oughta mean something. Do you know where we are?"

"Naw, man," said Andrew, "where are we?"

"This is Prince Edward County, man," said Dave. "The schools around here have been closed for four years. They ain't ever gonna open."

Dave gave a quick glance to Whitley before turning an intense look at Andrew.

"I don't think they like you being here, Andy."

On instinct, Whitley held up his hand and quickly called the players together into a gigantic circle.

"Look guys," said the team captain with a look of concern, "this is Prince Edward County, and you know what happened here. We don't need nothin to happen to Andy. Let's stay close around him and just slowly walk back to the bus, now."

The movement was quick and tight, Zongo and Whitley acting as Andrew's personal bodyguards, all eyes darting eerily around the strange town.

****

Inside the large restaurant, the players—four to a booth—talked quietly as they waited to be served. Andrew sat with Zongo, Ken, and Dave, reliving their chilling journey through downtown Lynchburg.

"Oh, man," said Ken, "was that scary or what?"

Andrew spoke above the laughter.

"I wasn't scared til I saw y'all get jumpy," he said, then explicitly made a point. "When da white boys git scared, it's time for da colored boy to git petrified."

As the laughter increased, Andrew became even more expressive.

"I was thinking," he loudly added, "Is this Lynch-Burg? Or Lynch-Heidelberg?"

Yet another roar.

With Andrew's humor at the center of the discussion, another teammate approached their booth with a newspaper.

"Hey Andy," he said, "I just picked up the Lynchburg newspaper. Look at this."

With his finger pointing to a photo, the player placed the newspaper in front of Andrew with Zongo leaning over to look. There was a picture of an E.C. Glass football player with both of his feet in a large tub of water, reading a newspaper. In bold letters, the caption read, "Bring Your Nigger."

Looking stunned, Andrew slowly announced the newspaper caption to those at his table.

"Bring ... Your ... Nigger," he said slowly. "Right in da newspaper." Zongo grabbed the paper.

"This is crap," he scowled.

"Damn," said Andrew, attempting to joke about the situation, "I thought people round here might be just a little more friendly."

Nobody laughed.

As the newspaper was passed to another table, Coach Moody walked up and stood beside Andrew. He leaned over and spoke quietly, although the others at the table could still hear.

"Andrew," said Moody, "they say that, uh ..."

The coach hesitated.

"They won't serve us as long as you're sitting out here."

Everyone at the table looked at Andrew and laughed as if Moody was trying to pull a prank. He wasn't.

"C'mon, coach, I know you're joking," said Andrew.

"I'm not joking, Andy. I'm serious. They say they won't serve us with you sitting in the dining room. They have a table set up for you in the back. They want you to eat in the kitchen."

The entire room turned quiet, players from all tables staring in disbelief at Andrew. There was a long silence, Coach Moody looking both apologetic and embarrassed.

"You're not joking," Andrew quietly said.

The coach somberly shook his head.

"No, Andy."

Andrew got up from the booth, head slightly bowed, and walked slowly toward the kitchen, the white restaurant manager standing with one arm holding the door open.

Entering the kitchen, Andrew saw a middle-aged Black woman and a tall Black man in his early thirties. Both were wearing white aprons and standing behind a table that was draped with an ironed tablecloth, well set, and stock filled with every food on the menu. Both were smiling proudly at him.

"Hello, son," said the woman. "We fixed up some good eatin for ya."

"Yeah," said the man, "sit right down."

"Yes sir," said Andrew as the man pulled out a chair for him at the table.

"If dere's anything else you want, honey, and you don see it, just ask, and we'll get it," said the kind woman.

Andrew sat down, but before he could begin eating, the kitchen door opened.

"Hey, Andy," said Whitley, walking in with Zongo. "We thought you might have something special goin on, so we came to eat with you."

"Yeah," said Zongo, "make some room."

"Y'all come on in and sit down right here," said the female cook.

The male kitchen worker scooted two more chairs to the table as Kenny and Zongo sat down. The three ate like kings, smiling and laughing in great conversation.

****

Dressed in road blue, the Norview Pilots were walking toward a misty, dimly lit field with hundreds of National Guard troops creating a path for them. Lynchburg's City Stadium, with its enormous wrought iron gates and stone walls, resembled an ancient castle.

As the players reached the entrance, they saw a stadium that, nearly an hour before kickoff, was already filled. No wonder the town had seemed empty. They also could not help but note that all eyes were glaring at them, obviously looking for Andrew. The line of Virginia National Guardsmen continued with a shoulder-to-shoulder wall between the stands and the field. They also were stationed at outposts throughout the stadium.

E.C. Glass was warming up on their side of the 50-yard line. They were not very tall, but thick and hard farm boys, a quick and a well-coached football machine. At first sight of the Norview players, the crowd erupted. The greeting was ugly, so noted by the broadcaster from Lynchburg's largest radio station.

"Welcome to what could be the game of the year," said the local sportscaster. "Tonight should be a thriller between two undefeated powerhouses, Lynchburg's own E.C. Glass Hilltoppers hosting the Norview Pilots, all the way from Norfolk. Having already smashed their first three opponents, the Hilltoppers know that the road to a possible state title could be decided right here against the 1-0 Pilots. One year ago, Glass and Norview tied 7-7 in Norfolk. Although they both won their districts and notched undefeated seasons, because of that one tie, neither could lay claim to the coveted state crown. Still, Norview has captured two state championships in the past three years and carries a 37-game winning streak, five straight Eastern District titles, and a six-year mark of 55-2-2. This, folks, is a true football dynasty."

The Pilots had gathered behind one of the goalposts, preparing to streak onto the field. The crowd's anger, already at a frenzy, seemed to be feeding upon itself, as if blood would not be enough.

"With kickoff about 10 minutes away, looks like about all of the 15,000 fans are already packed into sold-out City Stadium," continued the broadcaster. "We also have the presence tonight of nearly 1,000 National Guardsmen, sent by Governor Almond as a security precaution in light of the arrival of Norview's colored halfback, Andy Heidelberg, the first Negro to ever play white high school football in Virginia. Heidelberg is apparently the real deal, having broken the color barrier last week with two lightning touchdowns for the Pilots. He is joined in the Norview Y formation by Number 26, halfback Calvin Zongolowicz, and number 48, Ken Whitley, the returning first-team, all-state fullback, and state champion heavyweight wrestler. With Whitley hobbled by a knee injury, senior Matt Crawford, a starter at halfback on last year's team until being bumped this season by Heidelberg, should see plenty of action tonight at fullback. And here come the Pilots ..."

Again, the reception was hostile, the sound of the radio overpowered by the deafening boos and insults from the fiery majority. Only a small section of the stadium had Norview fans, including several busloads of students. Their cheers could hardly be heard against the home crowd's uproar.

After the opening kickoff, the Pilots looked somewhat shaky as Glass drove 80 yards on six plays for a touchdown.

"If that 200-mile bus trip left the Pilots a little tight, they had better loosen up quick," surmised the radio announcer as jeers and racial taunts continued to pepper the background of the broadcast. "Heidelberg, Norview's colored back, is deep to receive. Boy, there must be 10,000 catcalls in this stadium."

Andy received the kickoff at the five, skirting past several tacklers until being leveled at the 25. What followed was a late hit and several more Hilltoppers jumping the pile.

"I guess Glass is sending a message," chuckled the radio announcer. "But I don't see any flags."

Inside the pile, Andrew was being jabbed and ridiculed.

"You ain't nothin, nigger," snarled a Glass defender.

"Yo black ass is mine, nigger boy," said another.

"Piece of shit," added the first defender.

188

As the Glass players continued to poke and harass, some Norview players tried to pull them off the pile.

"Get outta here," a referee yelled at the Norview players. "Don't touch nobody."

"One more blue player gets involved in this and it's gonna be 15 yards," said another ref. "Back off."

As Dave Fitzgerald attempted to help Andrew stand, a defender intruded.

"Damn nigger lover," the Glass player bellowed into Fitzgerald's face.

In anger, Fitzgerald pushed the bigoted player away, the closest referee immediately grabbing for his flag and tossing it high in the air.

"That's 15 yards against blue," the referee commanded. "Unsportsmanlike conduct."

On the sideline, the Norview coaches were furious.

"You can't be serious," McClurg yelled at the nearest official as Andrew finally was able to stand, the cheering from the crowd turning to boos and more taunts.

As the Pilots lined up for their first play from scrimmage, the E.C. Glass defenders were talking trash.

"Hey, I got a nigger lover right here, boss," said the defensive tackle.

"Yeah, me too," said the nose tackle. "Didn't know Virginia had so many nigger lovers."

Senior quarterback Harry Wilkerson faked to Andrew and handed off the Zongolowicz, who busted off-tackle for a 17-yard gain. After the whistle, away from the play, Andrew was leveled by a blindside hit. A referee watched but did not pull his flag.

"Throw the flag," yelled McClurg. "You saw that!"

The official ignored the Norview coach.

As Andrew limped to the bench, the stadium again erupted

in cheers and boos.

"The colored boy appears to be shaken up," blared the radio. "Don't know why? He didn't have the ball. This Heidelberg is fast, but the jury is still out concerning his toughness."

Coach Brown approached Andrew.

"You okay, Andy?"

I'm fine, coach," said Andrew, a look of intense anger. "Cheap shot, that's all."

"Good, we'll get you right back in there in a minute."

By the second quarter, Norview had regained any lost composure. Despite some rather obvious hurdles, they could beat this team. Defensively, the game had turned even. Down by only a touchdown, the Pilots created several good drives, only to have them stall. With six minutes left in the half, they had marched to midfield.

"Pitch to Heidelberg around right," reported the radio. "He cuts inside, and he's found a hole. He's headed for the end zone. Touchdown. Wait, there's a penalty flag from behind Heidelberg, thrown rather late. The referees are huddling. Offside is now being signaled against Norview. Bring it back."

In an age without instant replay, the reality of the moment found the referee trailing Andrew, seeing the breakaway, then grabbing his flag. As other whistles backed up his whistle, the Norview bench exploded, the Glass fans going from a momentary gasp to loud cheers of relief and glee.

"What are you doing?" Coach Mac yelled at the officials. "That was clean all the way. How much of a home job can you throw?"

"Knock it off, coach," said one of the refs. "There was a penalty. Your team was offside."

"You called that after our runner broke away," argued McClurg, his eyes glazed in fury.

"Are you questioning our integrity, coach?" growled the

referee. "He had trouble getting his flag out of his pocket."

"He's not even the line judge," said McClurg. "He can't make that call. That's crap, and you know it."

"Watch your language, coach."

McClurg turned away from the official, his anger besieged by frustration.

"That's the way it's gonna be," he said to Coach Moody. "Unbelievable."

"The Norview coach, Charles McClurg, is quite unhappy with the call," rang the radio. "But you can wipe that touchdown off the board because somebody on Norview jumped the gun. I didn't see it up here, but the referees were right on top of it."

It would get worse ...

Again, a big gain by Andrew ended with a cheap hit after the whistle. As 33 was being punched and bitten beneath the pile, a fight nearly broke out. The Pilots were penalized for unsportsmanlike conduct.

And, for the second time, Andrew had a breakaway touchdown called back by a late flag.

Glass then scored its third touchdown, their fans in gleeful explosion, the Norview faithful sitting in stunned silence, the National Guard tightening its protection of the field.

When it was over, Norview had fallen 21-0, the 37-game winning streak now lost to history. As the teams lined up for the post-game show of sportsmanship, not one opposing player shook Andrew's hand, many using the moment for one more crude remark.

The long and silent bus ride back to Norfolk seemed to last forever, players busted and bruised, stunned and angry. Sitting next to Fitzgerald, Andrew silently kept replaying the game, certain the loss was entirely his fault. Perhaps, he thought, this was the very reason he had been cut the previous year. It was never about his talent. The coaches realized all along that the white South would never be capable of playing fair.

It was almost 3 a.m. when the bus arrived back at Norview. Coach Moody told the players to go into the gymnasium and take a seat in the bleachers, wait for Coach McClurg to dismiss them. They sat in the darkened gym, heads bowed in devastation, ruffled coats and ties, silence but for a stray sniffle, many still trying to hold back tears, all just wanting sleep, to somehow forget.

They waited.

Finally, Coach McClurg, followed by Moody and Brown, entered the gym from their office. Coach Mac stood in front of the team, waiting for all eyes to find him.

"We only meet in the gymnasium after a game when we lose," he said, hesitating to look through the crowd of drained faces. "I don't want to meet in here again."

He turned and left the gym.

The players sat in silence for a few more moments, finally realizing they could leave. Nothing else was said.

****

Sunday morning's *Virginian Pilot* had the bad news blazed across the top of the sports page—*GLASS STOPS PILOTS AND STREAK.*

Sportswriter George McClelland noted that, "almost from the opening kickoff, it was obvious that this would not be a typical Norview evening."

There were quotes from Coach McClurg, who had taken over the Norview program the Monday after its last loss, way back in October 1957. McClurg had been 37-0-2 as a head coach.

Gaines

Coach Mac, as would be expected, made no excuses to the press.

"It would have taken our very best game to beat Glass, and we were far short of that tonight," he said. "But there's no reason to get shook when you get beaten by a team as good as that."

Chapter 20

Two Burgers to Go

*A*t Barraud Park, Andrew was standing on the field as his junior players got ready for the game. Two of the players were fiercely arguing as they approached Andrew.

"Hey, coach," said the kid wearing jersey number 15. "Willie had number 33 last game, and he takes it again. He ain't got dibs on no special number. Can I wear it this game?"

"Boy, you gotta be quick in dis world," said Coach Heidelberg. "Next time be here earlier."

Problem solved. Andrew smiled and yelled for all his players to hear.

"Okay, team, bring it in; let's see who's ready to play some football."

****

At Warwick in the fourth game of the season, Andrew was back at his own goal line to receive a punt. Working on a one-game winning streak, the Pilots had apparently shaken the E.C. Glass debacle.

From the booth, WNOR's Bill Piersall called the action.

"We're midway through the first quarter in a scoreless game. The Farmers, on fourth-and-eight near midfield, will punt. It's a booming kick, fielded by Heidelberg at the one. Warwick has him surrounded as he retreats into the end zone. He's in trouble, gets away ... he outruns the first wave of Farmers. Heidelberg has found the sideline, there's a wall of blocking. Katie bar the door, he's at the 30, 40, midfield, Heidelberg's all alone ... goodbye ... 30, 20, 10, touchdown! Andy Heidelberg has just gone 99 yards ... he was never touched."

That proved the first dagger in a 33-7 Norview victory.

****

The following Friday at Foreman Field, the Pilots were again wearing road blue as they played cross-town rival Granby. Ahead 20-0, Norview's junior quarterback, Donald Stickland, pitched to number 33 with the intention of running out the clock ... which is exactly what Andy did.

"I used my hippy-dippy move to avoid some defenders," he would later tell the press. "I just kept on running. Next thing I know, I had a 66-yard touchdown on the final play of the game ... oops."

As Andrew was being congratulated by happy teammates and fans, he suddenly saw a heavy-set white man in his mid-thirties, wearing a fedora hat, running toward him in excitement.

"Lemme shake hands wit dat colored boy," the man yelled in glee. "Hey, young colored boy ..."

Andrew stopped as the "Hat Man" excitedly put out his hand. As they shook, the stranger placed a bill in Andrew's hand.

"Thank you, thank you," he gushed. "Boy, you saved my life tonight. That last touchdown of yours was the clincher. I beat the spread; I beat the spread!"

Heidelberg

With that, the "Hat Man" ran off the field, hooting and hollering. Andrew opened his hand to look at a $50 bill.

****

Standing in his living room, Andrew was stunned. He sensed this was coming, but what could he possibly do? She was too far away.

"Hey, I understand, Betty Jean," he said quietly into the phone. "Yeah, I know, you're busy, college is hard."

Andrew stared dejectedly as he listened, not really hearing or understanding, just knowing.

"No, it's okay," he said. "You don't have to explain. I gotta go now."

Andrew put down the phone and headed for his bedroom. Dumped by the girl he loved.

****

At Chittum Field, the Pilots were hosting the Newport News Typhoon. With Ken Whitley scratched from the offensive lineup due to a sore tendon, Matt Crawford had been given the start at fullback and responded with an early 11-yard touchdown run.

On the radio, Bill Piersall told his listening audience that Crawford was "undoubtedly the best second-string back in the Eastern District."

Later, Zongolowicz swept left and pitched to Heidelberg for a double reverse. Unfortunately, the Typhoon didn't bite. Seeing the trap, Andy simply stopped and headed the other way, now following Zongo, who leveled the final defender on a 33-yard touchdown run.

Despite being relegated to the defensive side of the ball because of a sore tendon, Whitley had another stellar game, including an interception near the Typhoon goal line. Returning the ball up the middle, Norview's middle linebacker plowed over three tacklers before being hit by two defenders at the five. But "The Bull" just kept moving, ultimately pulling his two tacklers over the goal line.

After Andrew notched a 57-yard catch-and-run touchdown, the radio audience were reminded of the obvious.

"The Pilots are unbeatable," Piersall commented. "And, by the way, Andy Heidelberg certainly has to be the story of Eastern District football."

****

After practice, Andrew was at his locker, changing into his street clothes. He was already a step late because his junior league team would be having a practice, so he would need to head directly to Oakwood Elementary. But, even in a hurry, Andrew was never the first one out of the locker room.

On this afternoon, most of the players had already left, but Andrew could hear Matt Crawford talking loudly to several of his school buddies from another row of lockers.

"Man, I must be the unluckiest guy in the world," Crawford said in a protruded voice, obviously aware that Andrew could hear.

"Unlucky?" said one of his friends. "Whatcha mean, Matt?"

"I been a starter since I was a sophomore," said Crawford, his voice booming through the locker room. "And in my senior year, I lose my startin position to a nigger. What kind of luck is that?"

Both friends agreed.

"It's crap," said one.

Andrew, who had almost finished dressing, leaned around the corner, resting his arm on the edge of the locker.

"Hey, Matt," said Andrew, as if they were best of friends. "Don't forget to tell em you didn't lose your position to just any nigger. You lost your position to a bad nigger."

As Andrew walked back to his locker, he could hear both of Matt's friends trying to contain their laughter. He also heard the slam of Crawford's locker door.

With a huge smile still plastered across his face, Andrew closed his locker and left to coach his junior team.

****

At the next day's Norview practice, Andrew once again marveled at the ferocious tackling ability of Kenny Whitley.

With the second-string offense pitted against the first-team defense, Matt Crawford rushed into the heart of the defense. At middle linebacker, Whitley devoured the runner as if it was a wrestling match.

"Oooohhh," was the resounding moan of the other players.

As Whitley helped Crawford back to his feet, Andrew moved up from the corner.

"Hey Whit, tell me how you do that?"

Whitley turned to Andrew with his distinctively sly smile and head slightly cocked, seemingly eager to offer a quick instruction in the art of wrap-around tackling and the wrestling takedown.

"It's easy, Andy. First, you get your center of balance with your feet slightly spread. Then just open your arms wide and brace for the hit. Let the runner go right into your chest, then wrap your arms around him and bull wrestle the sucker to the ground."

Andrew mimicked the technique, proud of his style.

"Nice, huh, Kenny? Next time they come up da middle, let em through and I'll take care of em."

"You think you're man enough, Andy?"

"Oh, you know I'm man enough, Kenny."

"Okay, but don't make me look bad by missing the tackle."

"Hey, man, I got it," bragged Andrew.

Whitley turned to the other defenders, who also were watching with amusement as the brash student learned from the all-powerful master.

"Okay, listen," said Whitley in the defensive huddle. "Next play they try though the middle, everybody lay off. Andy's gonna come up and show us his new tackling technique."

Everyone heartily agreed with the plan.

"Don't get hurt, Andy," kidded Fitzgerald.

"C'mon, man, you know I'm tough."

Dave smiled as he ran to his position at defensive end, calling out to quarterback Donald Strickland in the offensive huddle.

"Hey, Don, run that same play again. Andy wants to make the tackle."

"Okay," said Stickland. "You want a halfback or fullback?"

"Oh, he definitely wants me," yelled Crawford, who had the gift of being a punishing runner.

The two squads lined up. Strickland handed to Crawford, who blasted through a wide-open hole and directly into the path of Whitley, who casually stepped out of the way.

As advertised, Andrew held his ground and opened his arms. The rest was a blur. Crawford, pumped by power and an obvious dose of revenge, blasted right through the skinny defender, stepping on Andrew's chest as he tromped past.

Both sides roared as Whitley pulled Andrew off the ground.

"I shoulda told ya, Andy, to properly absorb the hit, you also need some meat on them bones."

Whitley cocked his head sideways, gave his sly smile, and popped Andrew playfully on his sore chest.

****

At Chittum Field, the Pilots were pounding the Cradock Admirals. Now starting at quarterback, Strickland handed off to Heidelberg, who was hit hard by a linebacker. Slow to get up, Andrew hobbled toward the sideline gasping for air and holding his rib cage, the team doctor meeting him halfway.

****

On Monday morning, Andrew, along with Zongo and Whitley, received an off-campus pass to visit Dr. Taylor.

"Damn, this is nice," said Andrew as he looked around the large medical office.

"Nice?" grumbled Whitley. "You try coming here every week to get your knee drained with that big needle. This ain't no picnic."

"C'mon, Kenny, you love the attention," kidded Zongo. "We get outta school early to come see Doc. Andy's right. This is nice."

Dr. Taylor entered the room.

"How y'all doing?" he said with a big smile.

He moved directly toward Andrew.

"Go ahead, Kenny," said the doctor, "you know what to do. Drop your pants to your ankles and get on the table. Andy, why don't you take off your shirt and let's get a look at those ribs. Zongo, I'll take a look at you in a minute."

"Hey, Doc," said Kenny, "I think Andy wants to get his knee tapped too. Show him the needle."

"Noooo, I don wanna see no needles," bellowed Andrew as he took off his shirt.

Zongo jumped into the conversation, his arms slowly and dramatically stretching out, as he talked, to show the mythical size of a gigantic needle.

"Andy," said Zongo, "don't tell me you're scared of a little needle."

"Hey, man, don't make me laugh," said Andrew, his hands holding his ribs.

The doctor moved Andrew's hands and methodically put his own fingers on the sore ribs.

"Okay, let's see the damage," Dr. Taylor said while pressing. "Tell me when it hurts."

"Oh, ooohh, oh yeah," Andrew cringed. "That's it."

"C'mon Andy," said Zongo, "be a man."

"Ah, ah, ah," Andrew groaned as the doctor removed his fingers from the battered rib cage, a look of concern.

"Andy, we're going to need an X-ray."

****

The next morning, Andrew entered Norview and casually walked up to the wall to be greeted by the jocks.

"Andy, I hear you're not gonna play Friday," said Fitzgerald.

"I'on know yet, man," said Andrew. "Doc told Coach I should sit out, but you know I ain't missin Homecoming. We gonna have a field day on Hampton. I gotta play."

"Well, even if you don't play, Andy, you can always go to the Homecoming dance," interrupted Zongo.

"Yeah," Andrew shot back, "and I'm gonna take your girlfriend, Karen."

"OOOOOhhhh," said every one of the jocks.

"Go ahead," said Zongo with a playful response. "She's way too much for me. She'll destroy you."

****

After practice, Andrew was heading south across the Norview campus. Zongo happened to be leaving at the same time.

"Hey, Andy, goin the wrong way, ain't ya?" he called from behind. "I thought you lived the other way."

Andrew stopped to wait for his friend.

"I do," he said, "but I gotta pick up a book for my dad at the post office."

"I'll walk with ya," said Zongo. "You might need a little interference goin this way. Hey, nice practice."

"Yeah, tell me about it," said Andrew, feeling to see if his ribs had gotten any better since the last time he checked. "All I did was stand around and watch y'all play."

"Yeah, you're good at that," joked Zongo.

"Man, I wanna be running that ball," said Andrew.

"You gonna be ready to play or what?"

"I'on know," said Andrew. "So, anyway, what happened to Karen today? She tired of you?"

"Naw, I'll get with her later. Hey, what about you? Ain't you supposed to be coaching that football team of yours?"

"Yeah, we practice after Norview's practice, but I gave the boys the day off. Man, we're good. We do all Norview exercises, and we run all Norview plays. Man, do they think um mean."

"So, you think you're Coach Mac, huh? Dress up for the game with your coat and tie? Wear that old-man hat?"

"Naw, man, I'm just myself."

"I wanna come to one of your games. I bet you ain't as good as you been bragging."

"We're even better," said Andrew. "Seven wins, zero losses. Undefeated."

"Don't remind me," said Zongo. "We should be unbeaten, except for that stupid Lynchburg game."

"Yeah, I ain't the best of luck for the team," said Andrew.

"What the hell you mean by that?"

"You know, we had a long winning streak until along came the colored guy."

"That ain't got nothin to do with us losin that game, you dork," said Zongo. "Kenny was hurt, the referees were shit, and Glass was pretty damn good."

As they arrived at the post office, Zongo pulled out a pack of cigarettes.

"I'll wait out here," he said.

****

Zongo was throwing his cigarette away when Andrew walked out with a package.

"I'm hungry," said Zongo, looking at the small restaurant next door. "Wanna get a burger or something?"

"What?" said Andrew. "You know I can't go in there, man."

"Aw, c'mon," said Zongo, "ain't nobody gonna say nothing. You and I are Norview football heroes."

Andrew was hesitant but went along with Zongo's assurance. C.J. opened the glass door, and they both entered, *Big Bad John* by Jimmy Dean blaring from the jukebox.

Andrew had never been in a white restaurant. There were booths on the right wall of the café, with a counter and stools on the left wall. Every customer looked up and stared as the boys approached the take-out counter.

Wiping his hands on a greasy apron, the cook walked from

the stove with a look of disgust.

"Gimme two burgers to go," said Zongo.

"We don't serve niggers in here," the cook grumbled.

"Good," said Zongo, "because I didn't order two niggers. I want two burgers."

"Get outta here, you wise-ass punks," snarled the cook, apparently not a football fan.

Once outside, Zongo offered his assessment of the situation.

"That fuckin asshole," he said.

"Yeah," said Andrew, "fuckin asshole."

Chapter 21

Homecoming

*I*t was midway through the first half on a sunny Saturday afternoon at Chittum Field, the stands packed and Norview with the early lead over Hampton.

On the sideline, Andrew was moving and jittery. Coach McClurg, wearing his game coat and tie with a fedora on his head, walked past.

"How're you feeling, Andy?"

"I think I can go, Coach."

"Your ribs feel okay?"

"Feel great, Coach."

McClurg smiled.

"Okay, get in there."

It took perhaps two seconds for Andrew to have his helmet on and be charging onto the field, applause becoming louder and louder with the realization he was in the game.

It would only take one play, Strickland throwing long to Heidelberg, who made a diving catch near the goal line. Ouch!

Pressing against his rib cage, Andrew was helped off the field by the trainer. Several minutes later, he was still moving slowly as Coach McClurg walked by.

"I'm okay, Coach," Andrew said.

"Andy, you're finished for the day."

A bit dejected, Andrew continued to move and stretch his body as Zongo reached the bench to take a break.

"You okay, Andy?"

"I'm fine. Coach says I'm done for today."

Zongo grinned.

"Hope that doesn't keep you away from the dance tonight," he said.

Andrew looked his friend in the eyes.

"Do me a favor, Zongo. If I get Homecoming King, bring me the crown on Monday."

****

Andrew, Zongo, and Whitley were walking down Tidewater Drive between several segregated neighborhoods, Kenny pointing in the direction of his home.

"I live over that way by the waterworks," he said.

"I live way back down the other way," said Andrew. "We almost neighbors, Whit."

Kenny smiled and pounded his fist into his open hand, then with two fists, pretended to wring something out.

"Thanksgiving morning, boys, we are gonna crush Great Bridge. We can chew on Wildcat in the morning, turkey in the afternoon. It's tradition."

"Say, Kenny," said Andrew, "since you mention Thanksgiving dinner, why don't you invite me over?"

Whitley turned his head to the side and gave that shy grin.

"Andy, this is the truth," he said. "I don't think my dad would have any trouble with it, but my momma would hit the roof."

"But, man," said Andrew, "I thought we were tight."

"Yeah, we are," said Kenny. "I'm just tellin ya."

"Don't worry about it, Andy," said C.J. "You can come over to my house for dinner any time."

"See, Whit, now that's what you call a friend," laughed Andrew. "I like that, Zongo."

"Oh, man," said Whitley, shaking his head.

****

Thanksgiving at Great Bridge, kickoff for the traditional meeting set for 9:30 a.m. In the locker room, the Norview players were dressed in their road blue uniforms.

"So, Andy, how's the ribs?" asked Whitley.

"They're fine, Kenny. I'm ready."

"You better be," said Kenny. "These guys are fast. We're gonna need your speed today."

"I'm so fast, they won't even notice me."

"Right," Whitely laughed as he turned to the team.

"Let's get ready, guys," he yelled. "We need to stick these turkeys in the oven and turn up the heat full blast."

****

It was a beautifully clear and cold late fall morning, the stadium at Great Bridge surrounded by woods.

"We've got a full house for the Eastern District showdown between the Great Bridge Wildcats and Norview Pilots," said Piersall to the radio audience. "Both teams bring 7-1 records to this Thanksgiving Day blockbuster. What a morning for football!"

It was, however, a bad day for Norview's number 33 ... four fumbles. The mocking by the opposition suddenly bothered him, their fans hurling the usual racial remarks that somehow stung a bit more.

The good news was that the Pilots escaped Great Bridge with a 9-7 victory.

As teammates congratulated one another in the locker room, Andrew sat at his locker and stared at his hands.

"Cut the sad face," said Whitley. "So, you dropped the ball a couple times. We still won, didn't we?"

"Yeah, we did, but I sure didn't do my part. I'on know, Kenny, I ain't never fumbled four times in my life. Damn, my ribs heal, and my hands get polio."

One last game to play ...

****

At the end of practice, the players huddled around Coach McClurg.

"It's been a memorable year, men," said the coach as he tugged on his baseball cap. "One left and it's the biggest. Gonna be a lotta people watching tomorrow night and only one team is gonna be the champion. Don't any of you think it's gonna be easy, it's not. Maury is good, really good, and they want this game. But if we play Norview football—hard-nosed, team focus, total desire, never quit—we win the league and district. Captains, you got anything to say?"

John Hughes moved to the center of the pack.

"Y'all know I've never liked Maury. Let's stomp em in the ground."

Whitley now stood beside him.

"They call their defense the snakes," said Whit. "Well, if that's so, then we're the mongooses. We eat snakes for dinner."

The team cheered as they came together as one. After breaking, Andrew walked with Whitley toward the locker room.

"Hey Whit, what's a mongoose?"

Whitley stopped walking, pulling back his head in surprise.

"Didn't you read *The Jungle Book*? Rikki-Tikki-Tavi? The mongoose kills the cobra?"

"Oh, yeah," said Andrew.

"Quick and sly, that's the mongoose," said Whitley. "Snakes don't stand a chance."

Chapter 22

December 1, 1961

*A*ndrew stepped onto Foreman Field, knowing this would be his last high school football game, knowing he must excel.

"Don't think about four fumbles," Zongo had told him. "Think about four touchdowns."

Both Norview and Maury were 8-1, the winner would be Eastern District champion, a title the Pilots had held for seven straight years.

Andrew looked up into the stands. He had never seen so many people at a football game, anywhere. Foreman Field held 30,000 and it was jammed to the brim, an equal distribution of Norview and Maury fans, plus about 7,000 black fans, each group claiming separate sections.

Until five days earlier, the game was to be played at Norview, but because of the significance and heavy demand for tickets, it was moved to Norfolk's historic stadium, site of the annual Oyster Bowl.

The Maury Commodores, snakes and all, came for war. Zongo notched the only touchdown in the first half, but as Bill Piersall mentioned more than once from his radio booth, "it was anyone's game."

Early in the third quarter, Norview struck again.

Taking an off-tackle handoff from Donald Strickland, Andrew spun away from a hit and broke outside for a 54-yard touchdown.

On the sideline, the coaches were trying to break up the festivities. They were two scores ahead, but there remained a full two quarters to play. This was no time to celebrate.

As the third quarter ended, with the Commodores facing fourth and goal, Andrew made a touchdown-saving stop to keep the shutout intact.

He would be mobbed by teammates.

"Way to go, Andy," yelled Whitley. "You're the mongoose."

That he was. A final score by Strickland on a keeper around left end and Norview notched an impressive 20-0 victory.

As the Norview fans—both races—rushed the field, Andrew and his teammates celebrated. Whitley gave Andrew a bear hug and Zongo pounded on his pads, Andrew returning the compliment before yet another hug.

And then it was over ...

****

On a cold December afternoon, Andrew was playing a pickup game of football with a group of friends, including Freddy, who was home from college. As always, the action was furious and the atmosphere cantankerously fun. Finally, it was getting too dark to continue.

"Man, I can hardly see the ball," complained Freddy.

"Must be all dat studyin you been doin," kidded Bobby. "Wrecked yo eyes."

"Yeah, maybe, Knuck," said Freddy. "I guess I better get home."

"C'mon, old man," blurted Bobby. "It ain't dat dark."

"Yo, Freddy," said Andrew, "I'll walk with you."

Bobby picked up the football.

"Next touchdown wins," he yelled at the remaining players.

"Next touchdown?" interrupted Andrew. "Without me and Freddy, you boys gonna be here all night."

"Hey, see ya tomorrow," said Bobby. "Y'all old men better go home and get under a warm blanket."

The two friends walked off the field, the game continuing in the background.

"So, Freddy, you like it in college?" asked Andrew.

"Oh yeah, it's cool. And I'm doing okay. What are you gonna do when you graduate, Bird?"

"I wanna go in the Marines, but my momma has other ideas," said Andrew. "Guess I might have to pick one of those colleges that been offering me a football scholarship."

"Where do you want to go?"

"I'on know, man. I got letters and scholarships from places I ain't even heard of ... at least 50 scholarships."

"What? You're kidding? Like, what schools?"

"Oh, man," said Andrew. "Ohio State, Michigan State, UCLA, Norfolk State, Grambling, Morgan State, Coast Guard Academy. You name it, I got it."

"Damn, Heidelberg, all the stories I heard must have been true."

"Oh yeah, I was good."

"I'm just sorry I never got home to see any of your games," said Freddy. "Everybody told me you were the big star at Norview, and my momma sent me the newspaper stories. How exactly did you do that?"

"It was not easy," Andrew said in a deep, slow voice.

"What about the halls?" Freddy said. "Man, I always hated the halls."

"Nobody gives me trouble anymore," said Andrew.

"You're kidding?"

"Naw, man," assured Andrew. "Everything changed soon as I made the football team. I went from shit to sugar in two seconds flat. Like Miss Perry said back in tutorin school, 'football rules the world.' She nailed that."

"I bet you caught a lotta shit from the other teams," said Freddy.

"Oh yeah, some real nasty shit, especially when I was at the bottom of the pile. Kicked, punched, stepped on, bitten ... they twisted me in every direction. And you should have heard all the names. Oh, I forgot, you have heard all the names."

Again, Freddy understood.

"Man," Andrew continued, "when we played Maury for the championship three weeks ago, one of their dudes bit me so hard I still got teeth marks on my leg. But, hell, that's football. I loved it."

"I saw that three Norview guys made All-State," said Freddy.

"Yeah, Whitley and Zongo made first-team, Hughes got second-team All-State. Shoot, man, Whitley made the *Parade* All-America. I tell you, man, all of them are great."

"But all that shit you did," said Freddy. "No awards? Nothing?"

A trace of bitterness crossed Andrew's mind.

"Yeah, even as good as I played against Maury and Granby," he said. "I rushed for more than 100 yards in each game and scored in both of them and didn't even get All-Foreman Field. Zongo told me I should have at least gotten All-Tidewater and All-District. I didn't even make All-City. Man, you know da score in Virginia. If you're white, you're all right; if you're Black, hey nigga, get back."

Chapter 23

The Best There Ever Was

J im Brown of the Cleveland Browns was standing at the podium before a capacity crowd in a makeshift banquet hall in the Ruffner Junior High auditorium. Seated at the head table, Andrew, like most in the room, considered Brown to be a football god.

"It's always hard in the NFL," Brown was telling the audience. "You get hit, you get knocked down, you get up. Just like life."

Brown glanced at Joe Austin, seated beside Andrew.

"Joe Austin, thank you, Mr. Riddick and the other esteemed businessmen of Norfolk and, of course, the Norfolk Recreation Bureau for inviting me to this great occasion," he said. "Thank you all."

As the guests stood to applaud, Austin took the mike.

"Jim Brown of the Cleveland Browns," said Austin in a brilliant master-of-ceremonies voice. "All-Pro running back, the best there ever was ..."

The applause and cheers continued as Brown raised his hand in thanks, the room finally quieting.

"We got another great football player here too," said Joe Austin. "Andrew Heidelberg, stand up and get over here."

The applause was deafening, almost as enthusiastic as the reception for the legendary Brown.

"Yes sir, Mr. Austin," said Andrew, keeping his distance from the microphone.

"Tonight, we want to pay tribute to Andrew Heidelberg with two special awards," said Austin. "Not everybody knows this, but Andrew coached the undefeated Colts to the junior championship."

The kids who played on the Colts certainly knew about their perfect season. They stood, hollered, and celebrated as the rest of the crowd joined, all smiling.

"What I don't know," Austin continued, "is how Andrew got those kids to listen to him. Because when he played recreation football, he never listened to Coach Beacoate or Coach Sears. He gave em fits."

The crowd burst into laughter, particularly Andrew's two former coaches, who jokingly shook their heads in agreement. Sears laughed so hard that his unlit cigarette fell out of his mouth and onto his plate.

"And, as we all know," Austin said, "Andrew also played a little football himself this past fall."

Now the crowd was really cheering.

"And what a wonderful season he had, on both offense and defense. Oh man, I was never surprised by his unbelievable touchdown runs. But his great defensive play was a shock. Because when he played in our league, I never saw him hit nobody ..."

Again, Austin sparked laughter.

"Well, we all saw how great he played for Norview High School. Andrew, you made history. But I gotta say this too, when the season ended and the newspapers selected the most valuable players and all-this and all-that teams, I didn't see Andrew's name. And some of those newspapers are represented here tonight, so all you reporters need to write this down. To present the 1961 Gridiron Club Award to the most outstanding high school player in Virginia, please welcome again the great Jim Brown."

Brown stepped back up to the podium with a gigantic trophy.

"Young man," said Brown, "everybody's been telling me what a great job you have done, and not just your football exploits. You may not realize this now, but even more important than football is the historic contributions made by you and all of the brave youngsters of the Norfolk 17 over the past four years for our civil rights. I know it has been a hard, hard battle. I know you have felt at times like you were out there standing all alone, but you've had company, son, all across the nation. It is an honor, Andrew Heidelberg, to present you with this prestigious award." Everyone stood and applauded as Brown handed the trophy to Andrew—*Most Outstanding Black Athlete in Virginia.*

"Wait a minute, folks," Austin said into the microphone. "Andrew, we have a special gift for you. Mr. Brown, would you do the honors?"

From a large cardboard box, the great Jim Brown pulled out a brand new Norview Pilots letterman's jacket, then helped Andrew try it on. It was a perfect fit.

****

Early June 1962, Andrew walked into the Norview cafeteria, a beautiful blue yearbook in his hand.

Andrew glanced around the room, smiling at the commotion of stories and laughter as the students exchanged their yearbooks. In the midst of the gathering, as if holding center court, he could not write fast enough, his own book receiving the words and autographs of nearly every senior in the room. He was just a "typical" high school student.

Well, not really ...

Andrew had not been called "nigger" by a Norview classmate, at least to his face, for his entire senior year. But he well understood that racism did not cave because of one great football season. He knew the dance—stay clear of the white girls, never drift into unsafe neighborhoods, maintain an inner vigilance.

Even more, he knew the other kids of the Norfolk 17 did not catapult to prominence because Andrew Heidelberg was scoring touchdowns. For them, life at a white school was still brutal, dangerous, hell ...

Change would be slow.

Chapter 24
The Anniversary

Andrew Heidelberg stood on the auditorium stage of Norview High School. It was February 2, 2009, exactly 50 years since that cold Monday morning he had dared enter the forbidden halls of the racist south.

"It was pure torture," said Andrew as the students gasped at the thought he was talking about their own high school, that their own grandparents lived in such a strange world, the white ghosts of massive resistance now expunged in disgrace.

Not that racism was dead. Every kid at Norview—no matter the race—understood that prejudice still existed. But they also realized how different were their lives from the seven old people gathered in front of them, the original group of kids who bravely brought integration to Norview just half a century back.

"Thank you for all you've done and everything you had to endure," said the student president.

"These people are legends," proclaimed another student, as if the seven old folks on stage were rock stars.

It was emotional, the applause deafening.

"What a difference," said Johnnie Rouse.

"It's overwhelming," added Carol Wellington.

Oddly, this marked the first time the seven had been in each other's company at Norview High. They had never sat down for lunch in the cafeteria, met after class, gossiped in the halls. Most days, they had not even seen one another.

During the first weeks of 2009, as festivities stretched throughout Virginia, Andrew and the thirteen other living members of the Norfolk 17 had often been together, sharing accounts all too similar. Some had not been back to Hampton Roads since leaving high school, some had chosen never to talk about the traumas they had tried so hard to forget. At first, their words were guarded. It was tough, intense, moving. But, despite the emotional scars, they carried a unique bond—from the early days in the basement school to their solo walks into hell, nearly trampled by hatred and fear.

"For three years, it seemed like I was called 'nigger' a thousand times every day," Andrew told the students at the 50th anniversary. "I was hurt, angry, and numb. But they were not going to make me quit. That played on my heart every day ... you cannot quit."

From the crowd, the Powerful Pilots' long-time wrestling coach, Ken Whitley, smiled as his good friend spoke, remembering that one ironic twist in the bloody history of bigotry, when the white kids of Norview found that they actually liked the skinny "colored" halfback ... his personality, his fight, his character.

Near the gymnasium door, there's a large photo on the wall of the 1961 Norview Pilots football team, Eastern District Champions. It's quite easy to locate number 33. He's like "a fly in buttermilk."

Andrew Heidelberg was a pioneer ...

Dedicated to the Norfolk 17

Teachers, doctors, writers ... each a great American sharing a story of courage and grace.

Norview High School: Olivia Driver, Patricia Godbolt, Freddy Gonsouland, Andrew Heidelberg, Delores Johnson, Johnnie Rouse, Carol Wellington.

Granby High School: Betty Jean Reed.

Maury High School: Louis Cousins.

Norview Junior High: LaVera Forbes, Edward Jordan, James "Skip" Turner, Patricia Turner, Claudia Wellington.

Blair Junior High: Lolita Portis, Reginald Young.

Northside Junior High: Geraldine Talley.

Johnnie Rouse (left), Carol Wellington, and Andrew leave Norview on Feb. 2, 1959.

Alone in the cafeteria

Heidelberg

Betty Jean Reed at Granby

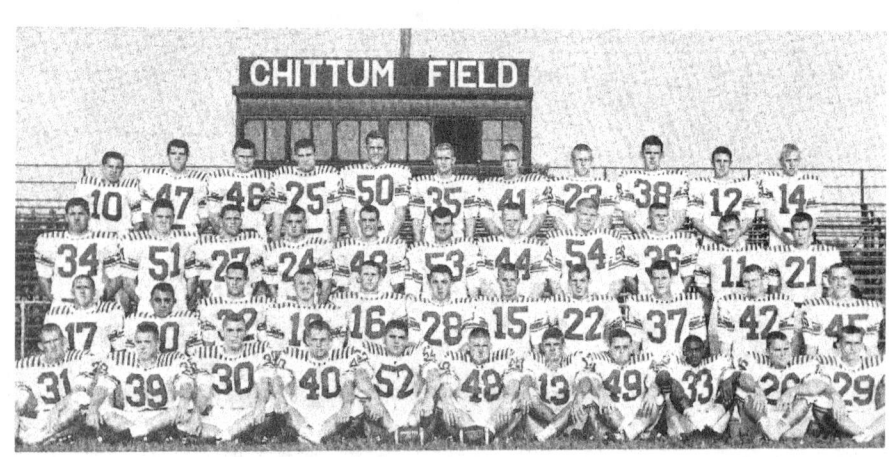

1st ROW: L. to R.: J. Stafford, I. Bishop, W. Weaver, R. Toldstedt, J. Hughes, K. Whitley, H. Wilkinson, C. Mullins, A. Heidelberg, C. J. "Zongo," R. Nelson. *2nd ROW:* T. Futch, G. Reyes, D. Mutter, B. Boyd, P. Piercy, T. White, D. Priddy, D. Strickland, M. Barnette, S. Morson, D. Fitzgerald. *3rd ROW:* J. Rothgery, S. Hufton, G. Ellenburger, W. Foshay, R. Phipps, A. Simmons, B. Dozier. R. Goodson, W. Davis, R. Spruill, J. Mizzell. *4th ROW:* W. Smith, L. Bice, C. Naprstek, J. Collier, T. OKonck, B. Elliot, M. Rockwell, G. Cartwright, B. Houston, M. Steele, B. Grillo.

1961 Norview Pilots

Gaines

Andrew Heidelberg and C.J. Zongolowicz

Ken Whitley

Heidelberg

Andrew signs to play football at Norfolk State.

Gaines

The old backfield:
Heidelberg, Whitley,
and Zongolowicz

Andrew and Patricia Turner

Civil Rights activist

Biography

Andrew Irwin Heidelberg was born on November 6, 1943, in Norfolk, Virginia to Lena and Colonal Heidelberg. At the age of fourteen, he joined sixteen other Black students (The Norfolk 17) to integrate six all-white schools.

In 1961, during his senior year at Norview High School, Andrew became the first Black athlete to play varsity football at an all-white public school in Virginia and the South. From 1962-66, he attended Norfolk State College, majoring in chemistry and biology, breaking into the starting lineup with the Spartans in his freshman year. After college, he signed as a free agent with the Pittsburgh Steelers, and later played in the Atlantic and Continental football leagues. His athletic accomplishments were notably mentioned in the Pictorial History of the Colored *Intercollegiate Athletic Association (CIAA) Professionals 1950-1984*, written by A. B. Whitfield. In 2015, he would be inducted into the Hampton Roads African American Sports Hall of Fame.

Andrew (left) and his brothers

In 1967, Andrew changed focus and entered the banking industry. At the Industrial National Bank of Providence, he became the bank's first Black branch manager, credit officer, and commercial loan officer. In 1976, he and a friend founded Heidelberg, Clary & Associates, Inc., the first 100 percent Black-owned and operated firm performing major contracts for the U.S. Environmental Protection Agency. Heidelberg was president and CEO of the firm. He later worked at Barclays Bank of New York and Banco de Ponce-New York as a vice president and corporate manager.

Retiring in 1999, he returned to Norfolk State University to earn a B.S. degree in interdisciplinary studies. He went on to serve as assistant treasurer and chief deputy treasurer for the City of Hampton, Virginia. Retiring again, Heidelberg became a popular public speaker, appearing in numerous television events, panel discussions, and lectures across the nation about the impact of The Norfolk 17 in fighting racism.

In 2005, Heidelberg was selected by Governor Mark Warner to serve a two-year term as a member of the Brown v. Board of Education Scholarship Awards Committee. He was appointed to serve two additional terms (through 2011) by Governor Tim Kaine. In 2006, he published *The Norfolk 17: A Personal Narrative on Desegregation in Norfolk, Virginia in 1958-1962*. He later collaborated with Robert D. Gaines to write a movie screenplay and book they agreed, at that time, to call *The Colored Halfback*.

Andrew Heidelberg served faithfully as a deacon at Temple Beth El in Suffolk and resided in Hampton with his wife, Luressa, before departing this life on July 6, 2015. His two daughters, Angela Roldan and Kirsten Heidelberg, both graduated from Norview, the school he integrated. He had three stepsons—Stephone, Isaiah and Judah—and a beautiful granddaughter, Miss April Lucinda Roldan.

Robert D. Gaines

Born into a naval family in 1945, Bob Gaines was raised in California, Rhode Island, and Virginia. Even as a child, he had an obsession for recording his stray thoughts into hundreds of notebooks.

He attended Norview High School from 1959-62, moving before his senior year to Long Beach, California. After graduating from San Diego State University, Bob would spend a decade as an award-winning sports columnist before moving east, eventually retiring from Bucknell University in 2012.

Heidelberg is the sixth book he has had published— *The Three Mathewsons* (Hidden Shelf Publishing House 2012); *The Christian Gentleman: How Christy Mathewson's Faith and Fastball Forever Changed Baseball* (Roman & Littlefield 2015); *Loose Chronicles: Dog from a Distant Universe* (Hidden Shelf 2017); *One Christmas Lasts Forever* (Hidden Shelf 2018); and *The Brave Historian* (Hidden Shelf 2021).

Acknowledgments

Most of all, I thank Andrew Heidelberg ... for his character, strength, humanity. He refused to take a back seat in life.

The long list of amazing people who helped to get the word out about this important piece of history was fueled by Randy Wright. From the Norview Class of 1965, Randy served as a Norfolk City Councilman from 1992-2010 and gladly introduced me to a number of amazing people.

Thank you so much to:

Kenny Alexander
Brenda Andrews
Joan Ewell Brookes
Leonard Colvin
Paul Fraim
Chip Frasier
Lisa Godley
Luressa Heidelberg
Kevin Kaiser
Adale Martin
Harry Minimum
Regina Mobley

Cassandra Newby-Alexander
Paul Rubin
Karen Rudd
Patricia Turner
Colin Warren-Hicks
Denise Watson
Ken Whitley
Karen Sherman Whitley
Randy Wright
Arlene Wright
Frank Ziggenfuss

Thanks also to:

City of Norfolk Government
The Norfolk 17
Norfolk Public Library
Norview Alumni Association
Norview High School
Norfolk State University
Old Dominion University

Explore the Hidden Shelf